CIRCUMNAVIGATING
LOW KEY

CIRCUMNAVIGATING
LOW KEY

*Where a small boat and a smaller budget
lead to big adventure*

CAPTAIN
WOODY HENDERSON

SHERIDAN HOUSE

Published 2010 by
Sheridan House Inc.
145 Palisade Street
Dobbs Ferry, NY 10522
www.sheridanhouse.com

Library of Congress Cataloging-in-Publication Data

Henderson, Woody.
   Circumnavigating low key : where a small boat and a smaller
budget lead to big adventure / Captain Woody Henderson.
      p. cm.
   ISBN 978-1-57409-299-8 (pbk. : alk. paper)
   1. Boats and boating. 2. Sailing. 3. Single-handed sailing. I. Title.
   GV775.H46 2010
   797.1—dc22   2010022802

ISBN 978 1 57409 299 8

Printed in the United States of America

Table of Contents

Introduction

It is one of my earliest childhood memories—watching a cartoon movie of an Indian boy living happily in the wild. On the big screen was our hero, larger than life, and all he needed for his adventures were his bow and arrow and a deerskin canoe. The seed had been planted.

I was lucky to be introduced to sailboats at an early age. I was probably ten when a friend showed me how to rig and sail his family's tiny Sabot. After that, I would often ride my bike down to the marina, hop the fence, rig the little dinghy and sail around the harbor on my own.

In eighth grade I had two posters on my wall. My friends' posters were of their favorite rock groups. One of mine was a beautiful aerial view of what I would later learn was Bora Bora. The other was of Heather Thomas. I didn't know where that island was and I didn't care. I wanted to be there . . . with Heather Thomas.

After high school I bought a 23-foot sloop with my roommate. I used to take her out solo on stormy days, hoist all the sails, lash the tiller and sit up by the mast. With the stereo cranked and a coldy in hand, I would sing out of tune as loud as I could while the boat thrashed about in wave-driven chaos.

It took most of my teenage years to figure out that a traditional life wasn't going to do it for me. I was having my share of success. I owned a miniblind business and had an apartment

on the beach. I had a convertible Bronco, the ski boat, a sailboat and the hot girlfriend. I lived like a rock star and could
want for nothing—until my roommate Scott moved to Hawaii.

It wasn't that I wouldn't be able to rent his room, the waiting list was long (if not at all distinguished). What plagued me
was how a person could just up and move to another state. I
asked him and discovered that indeed he could just pack up his
tools and find the same framing jobs in Hawaii. This had me re-
flecting on my life. I had avoided marriage and kids (I was only
23!). I was as free as anyone. And I kept telling myself that. It
wasn't true though. My business was like a family. I had clients
and suppliers and crew. I was just as anchored as my married
friends (without the benefit of the mini fan club). The world
closed in on me.

It was then that I decided the 23 footer was not my dream-
boat. At the other end of King Harbor were two big piratical
ketches. I used to ride my bike over to sit and stare at them. I
decided that these were real sailboats. They probably had been,
and would again be, sailing the seven seas on globe girdling,
swashbuckling adventures. They were sailboats with multiple
masts, long stretches of varnished wood and decks of teak.
They had sweeping bows and intricately carved decoration that
worked its way aft. At the stern were those bitchin pirate windows that belied the large master's quarters—the lair of an ex-
plorer. These boats breathed adventure.

I would later meet Dan who owned the one called SAGA.
Her name said it all. The other boat, even more the pirate ship,
was called LOST SOUL. Bigger even than SAGA, LOST SOUL was
dressed out in black trim. Her varnish was darker, her masts
taller, her name emblazoned in gold-leaf script on each side of
the bow and looked even grander on the stern. She flew a large
Jolly Roger, high up in her heavy stays. I didn't know anything
about LOST SOUL but I wanted to believe she had been around.

Trapped by my business and the life I used to want, I began
to scheme. I saw myself traveling by sea to exotic ports, engag-
ing strange natives and sampling the local fare. I jumped all in
with the first plan that came to mind. My day job was flexible

and so I took an evening job as a bartender at a yacht club (combining my interests). My friends who bartended made tons of money. I figured it was a social job that I could get anywhere in the world so I could replenish funds between my grand adventures. I was planning to give up everything I had for the freedom to cruise the palm tree-lined, white sand beaches of our blue planet. Of course, I had no idea at the time that bartending was a minimum wage job with little or no tips in most other countries.

A new restaurant/bar closer to home offered me a job and I took it. One of the bartenders there had just gotten back from cruising the South Pacific in a sailboat! Jody had actually been to the island I spent my childhood dreaming about, Bora Bora. For the Fourth of July, Jody and her boyfriend invited the bar staff out for a sail. Jody said their boat was easy to find and its name was LOST SOUL.

Things were looking up for my world sailing voyage plan. With my bar job I figured I was deep into acquiring the necessary skills to provide traveling income for my "cruising" adventure and now I was being introduced to my first real cruisers. It was a great opportunity to learn some things about the lifestyle I wanted to live. They had been where I wanted to go, and on my dream boat no less.

As my bar friends partied aft, I sat out on the bow sprit watching the sun go down, the boat heaving beneath me on the big Pacific swell as her giant sails drew her powerfully through the sea. The only sound was of the ocean being pushed aside by the majestic bow. It wasn't like any experience I had ever had— a large stately object gliding so easily through the water with just the power of the wind. The experience made the stories of Drake, Magellan and Teach live in me again.

It was there near the bow that I met Bob Bitchin. He was the one responsible for everything LOST SOUL was. This guy was the real deal: 6'4", covered in tattoos (both nautical- and biker-themed) and wearing a black biker cutoff shirt. I told him he was an ass for having everything that I wanted. He just smiled. Later, I offered to work on his boat in exchange for the sheer pleasure of being around it and also to learn about ocean voyaging. The biker and his lady invited me to crew on their next adventure to the Mediterranean. I accepted, not knowing or caring what I was going to do with my business, toys, apartment etc. Essentially, my entire current life had to be tossed over the rail.

That year-long adventure led to other ocean voyages including a nine-month crew gig crossing the Pacific with the Raja Muda of Selangor. I got my Coast Guard Captain's license which vaguely qualified me to skipper boats. This attached a real income to doing what I loved. Once again, Bob Bitchin stepped in and hooked me up with my first skipper's job on a 75-foot luxury trawler yacht for wealthy owners. We refit the boat and I skippered her for a season along the Mexican Riviera. I learned a lot from the professional yacht maintenance crews who worked on the refit. The owner had given them specific instructions that they were to make sure I understood how to operate and repair every system onboard. I thank those owners for that invaluable experience.

From there I got into boat deliveries and skippering pleasure cruises to the islands off California until I found myself on another yacht. LADY A was a 76-foot sailing sloop. I skippered her up the Pacific Coast and around western Canada for the summer season with wonderful owners onboard. It was on that serene excursion that I began to feel like there was something missing. This wasn't my childhood fantasy. I was 33 years old and getting paid to travel on boats but I had given up my dream of doing it on my own boat, on my own terms. Besides that, these high-dollar ultra-safe cruises lacked, by my definition, true adventure. Something I discovered while working on yachts was that rich people had the same problems that the rest of us had; only theirs were compounded by their collection of stuff. Money had gotten in the way for them just as the pursuit of it was standing between me and bliss. Redirecting my focus, I searched for a way to get back on track.

I owned a sailboat at the time. She was a mess. I had gotten an incredible deal on LOW KEY, paying just $4,300 for the moldy little 33-foot sloop. She was stripped down and gutted when I found her sitting in a back lot, collecting rain. On the upside, the previous owner had kept and cataloged most of the old gear needed to reassemble her. He had planned to do a full refit so he could sail around the world, but, as it does, life jumped in and lured him off course. All the project needed was an eager captain—and crew.

On the first mate front, I was set. Dena was a little crazy. That is to say it only took a couple minutes to convince her to take a furlough from work and sail off into the sunset with me. So we made a plan. Instead of saving up for a real cruising boat, we'd fix up the coastal boat I had and see how far we could get. My last few boat jobs had left me with a small pile of cash. As it turned out, my 20k in savings would be just enough to get LOW KEY back into her coastal cruising form with one or two cruising essentials tossed in. We would keep it simple, both to keep the boat low maintenance, and because that's what the meager cash stash mandated. The most important lesson that I learned from yachting was that all the extra gear that goes on yachts to increase comfort had just the opposite effect on cruising boats which lack a full-time systems engineer. And as Dena was big on camping, I figured simplified cruising would be a step up that might suit her just fine.

Our schedule was tight: We had just four months to get the whole boat put back together before hurricane season arrived— a nearly impossible challenge for a landlubber but plenty of time for a boat maintenance expert and his trusty tool-handing, speed-varnishing sidekick. We plowed through the never-shrinking work list. Sea air being as fertile as it is, projects seemed to spawn other projects. Our departure date got pushed forward a month and we enlisted the help of friends. Our end of the dock was a slew of working bodies, dust and power tools, beer and tequila shots (in which the boys expected to be paid). The projects we did not complete got stowed away, with all their respective parts, into the bowels of our little floating experiment. And finally, when our friends stopped throwing us goodbye parties, we cast off for ports unknown.

CHAPTER 1

The Adventure Begins

I looked up at "The Hill." Every community has one, a town nearby where the cars are a little shinier, the yards a little bigger and the homes a little nicer. For us it is "The Hill," a green peninsula where the other half live. We regularly sail around their peninsula to get to our island paradise, Catalina. I have often thought how great it would be to live in one of those nice homes overlooking the sea. But not today. I leaned back in my beanbag, tiller in hand, heading south on our freshly refit little cruising boat, relishing the thought of our coming adventures. Not today. If one of those people were looking down at LOW KEY and knew that this little boat was sailing off to a hundred foreign ports and magical island destinations unknown, I think, maybe, they would want to be where I live for a change.

With the seeking of adventure often comes the odd challenge. The fond good-byes were still fresh in my mind when the engine came to an abrupt stop. Dena and I had just put the Volvo two-cylinder diesel into the boat the week before. Fossil records indicate that identical engines to mine were found lying alongside T-Rex and his ilk. During dock trials, the engine had often died. It was usually because of residual air in the new lines, but this sounded different. It sounded like it had been forcibly stopped. We had been working so hard for so many weeks, I could feel my sense of humor, which is closely tied to my unfounded optimism, starting to fade.

I took a deep breath and had a look around. I looked over the side for lines in the water that could have gotten fouled in the prop. Nothing. I looked in the *ER* (the engine room) and checked the prop shaft there. The shaft was dry, which meant the packing gland was too tight. The packing is a seal around the prop shaft that lets some water in to cool itself. If it is too tight, water cannot get in and the packing heats up, swells and clamps down on the prop shaft like a vice. I loosened it up to a drip, tightened the lock nut, and we were on our way again.

And then, the most amazing thing happened. Nothing broke, for what seemed like forever. The reality of where we were and what we were doing started to sink in. The months of hard labor were behind me. I relaxed a bit and let myself bask in the feeling. It was a warm feeling of freedom and anticipation of adventures to come. The payoff was finally here.

The first couple of days of our passage south from Southern California were spent motoring through light to no wind. In a sunny glassy calm, somewhere off northern Baja I decided to realign the big diesel. We shut her down. We were getting a little prop shaft vibration and I wanted to eliminate all possible sources. I had aligned the engine when we put it into the boat about a week before but the engine beds were new and could have settled, or the mounts could have compressed a little.

Engine realignment can be a pretty big job and not one you should be doing at sea, but it was one of those perfect calm days. There was not a whisper of wind, the water was mirror flat and the only movement was now and then, from the gentle wake of a passing ship somewhere far away. Dena stripped down and basked in the Mexican sun while I, somewhat distracted, went to work. To align an engine you adjust each of the four mounts up or down and side to side, until the engine flange meets up perfectly with the shaft flange by way of feeler gauges. I have done it a couple of times and it still seems like witchcraft to me, but after a couple of hours, it lined up and we were underway with a smoother ride.

And of course, to get the engine all tuned up and ready to

run was the best thing I could have done to get the wind to come back. We only had about 10 knots of wind that night but it was just enough. I put up the oversized headsail we call "the whomper" and shut the engine down . . . finally. Before we left California, Guillermo the diver came over for a last minute prop change/bottom cleaning. With a slippery hull and a flat sea, the fully loaded LOW KEY sailed swiftly along. The lights of Mexican towns off our port side slowly moved aft.

LOW KEY has an Aries wind steering system. Via an assortment of aluminum tubes and fittings, lines, blocks, a fin in the water and a wing in the air, this contraption steers the boat. Since I had never effectively used wind steering, it took some trial and error to get it right. Once set up I would sit and watch its magical dance with the elements. By our third day out, I had the sails, lines, and rig dialed in the way I like it.

I started the engine to charge the house batteries and noticed the alternator was not charging. The boat was sailing so well I really didn't care, and because most of the electrical system was still in boxes, we were not consuming all that much. Before leaving I had bought and installed a new set of golf cart batteries but had not yet felt the need to switch over from the old ones. This allowed us to be a little casual about potential battery damage. It took six days to draw the volts down near 12, a level that finally inspired me to attempt the alternator repair.

As I understood it, an alternator needs a little electricity to start charging. With a screwdriver, I shorted two of the contacts on the back of the alternator. It started charging. Great! I hooked up a lighted switch to the contacts and voilà, alternator control. An added bonus to this setup was that I could leave the switch off for no-load engine starting.

We had made it half way down the Baja peninsula and were coming up on our first scheduled stop, Turtle Bay. There were a few reasons we had planned to stop. 1) I tend to consider the worst case scenario and so if we had to motor the whole way we would have to pull into Turtle for fuel. 2) I figured I would be excited to get our first cruising leg behind us. 3) Last, but certainly not least, I didn't want Dena's first sailing experience, with night watches and everything, to be a long drawn out one. Especially if it was not going well for her. With that list in mind, the boat had been sailing well since Day Three, so we did not need fuel. Dena was loving her first voyage at sea and was talking about what she would cook in the coming days (and it sounded pretty good). We finally fired up the brass oil lamp which made the inside even more warm and cozy. The boat was hitting eight knots from time to time, the stars were amazing and we did not want to waste such great sailing. We stayed offshore and continued past Turtle on our blissfull sail south to paradise.

Attacked!

Late that night Dena was "attacked." I was just coming up for my watch when I heard Dena screech and then, in her animated way exclaim, "Oh my god, something hit me!"

I tried to console her, "O.K., O.K., I'm sure it was just . . ."

"It was kelp!! It hit me here!" and she pointed to the shoulder of her foulies, "and then here!" and she pointed to her cheek, "and then went down there" and she pointed down to the gear stored on the floor of the cockpit. I started to look for the offender. She asked me what I was doing and I had to break the news to her that kelp didn't just jump out of the water, that it was probably a flying fish or a squid. I added that we needed to find it before we forgot about it and it started rotting in our stern rode. She did not believe me until we found the little attack squid. They are drawn toward light so I think that maybe he was aiming for the reflector on her jacket. The next couple of mornings, we would find squid all over the boat.

The further south we went, the more wind we seemed to get. To counter-act the pressure extra wind puts on sails, we reef them down which reduces the area of the sails. As we approached Cabo San Lucas, we were fully reefed; a double reef in the main and our smallest headsail up. Dena was not one to volunteer her feelings. I'm not entirely sure she always knew what they were herself. Pathologically fearless, Dena would later confide in me that the only time she felt afraid on the entire crossing of the Pacific was while sailing off Cabo. She wasn't afraid for herself, she feared for *my* safety. The sailing approaching Cabo was a squally mess. As one would expect when rounding a massive cape and sailing into a warmer area, we had fluky winds that jumped around the compass, varying in force from 15 to 30 knots. This is all fine and easy going if you want to reef deeply once and are willing to go slow through the lighter airs. But where is the fun in that? Every time we would emerge from a squall into lighter wind I would shake out the reef so we could keep up our speed.

LOW KEY did not have cockpit-controlled reefing (properly set up boats have slab-reefing mains and roller-reefing headsails). To reef the main I would leave the safety of the cockpit and go out on deck to the mast. To reef the hank-on headsail I had to change out the sail altogether. This meant going out to the bow. Getting to the pointy end required sliding across the upturned dinghy. A lot of sailors recommend a harness for this type of thing (and you should wear yours!). I find them very restrictive. In my mind, manually reefing sails was old school Magellan style and it added to the adventure of the trip.

There were times I needed Dena to hand steer while I worked the deck. Of course they weren't the sunny calm times, they were the pitch dark night times with wind and rain blowing sideways across the deck. In those conditions my muffled shouts of, "Turn to port, turn to starboard" were not always properly translated. Tiller steering complicated matters, and we soon discovered that a better system, in those early times, was for me to yell, "Push" or "Pull." *Nessie*, our windpilot named for her lanky grey resemblance to the Loch Ness Monster, loved the wind—the more the better. Nessie took it all in stride, achieving MVP status. We were averaging eight knots of boat speed with forays into the 11s and 12s on swells. I checked the GPS the next morning. Sometime during the night it had recorded a 15.0. It must have been on Dena's watch because the highest I saw was 13.3. At the time I was pretty stoked about it. I asked her about the new record. She looked up from her book and said, "Really? Is that fast?"

On our ninth day out, we sailed merrily into Banderas Bay. There are two marinas near Puerto Vallarta—Nuevo Vallarta and Marina Vallarta. Our friend, Dave, on the cat JANE O, was rumored to be parked in Nuevo Vallarta so we sailed by there first and gave a call on the radio. We could not raise him, so we sailed on to the more familiar to me, Marina Vallarta.

It was Saturday, so I expected the office to be closed. My plan was to just park where we wanted and have them move us later. I gave the marina a courtesy call on the VHF, just in case, and an American sounding guy came back, asking about our boat length, etc. He sounded familiar. "Is this Karl?" I asked. "My name is Woody. I met you last time I came through here, years ago. I was on a boat called LOST SOUL."

There was a pause and then, "There's no room in this marina for a friend of Bob Bitchin." That's when I knew we were among friends.

We were coming up on hurricane season, so the marina was empty of other cruising boats. Karl met us at the dock. He set us up with a slip near a like-minded sailor named Dave (Dave #2), who was cruising his ketch SPERANZA. Dave was on another boat working. Karl called him on the radio and told him about his new neighbors and asked him if we could borrow his bathroom key (for our cherished arrival shower). Dave responded much like Karl, "I'm not lending my keys to anyone who hangs with Bitchin."

Arrival euphoria

At sea, on the trip down, there was a lot to watch for. With so much untested gear, we had to keep an eye on everything. I was adjusting and readjusting systems, rigging, and sails all the time. No one wants their maiden voyage to go awry. That kind of constant vigilance can be taxing. But now we had arrived! It was our first cruising destination! Boat and crew had come through with flying colors! The pressure was off and it was time to chill out and acclimate ourselves to the land of *mañana*.

Neighbor Dave showed up around sundown in a little Boston Whaler full of tools and a Pacifico on the dashboard (my cerveza of choice). He had stopped in Puerto Vallerta to make a little money before heading out cruising again. He worked on boats. We had questions about our new digs and Dave had answers and coldies for us. He gave us a shower key and the 411 on the CBT (location of the cheapest beer in town). We got cleaned up and walked over to a little place he had recommended for dinner at the west end of the marina. It was called Victor's.

We learned quickly that at Victor's, when you ordered a beer, they also brought you a shot of tequila. Every time. For one dollar, you got an 11oz. bottle of Pacifico and a shot of rotgut home-grown tequila! Welcome to Mexico. I could see how this place could trap someone less wary. Karl and his squeeze were just leaving the little restaurant when we got there, and he was good for a round.

We took the next day off and just walked around surveying our new surroundings. We left our first check-in/immigration/etc. to Karl who did that kind of thing. As would become our normal arrival procedure, Dena searched out the local produce stands while I followed along, mentally cataloging the yacht hardware and other locally accessible boat services.

Walking around can tire you out in the hot midday, so we hopped into the dinghy and putted over to Dave's afternoon hangout, Desperados, by the fuel dock. The fuel dock in Marina Vallarta overlooks the narrow waterway which leads to the 500-slip marina. The fuel dock in any marina is a great place to people and boat watch. For those of you living near a lake, it's like sitting above the launch ramp. For many a boater, the tight-quarter maneuvering can be very disconcerting. For those watching, it can be a quality source of entertainment. To enjoy the spectacle from the comfort of a patio chair, at a table under an awning, where 90-cent Pacificos were being served by a dusky latin senorita—well, that's just heaven. Desperados was owned by a Texan. The food was, you guessed it, Tex-Mex, and was real good. During our week in Puerto Vallerta, we were known to stop by on occasion.

We finally did track down our friend Dave #1, from the cruising cat JANE O. He took us downtown to show us *his* Puerto Vallarta. It was a great day of eating, drinking and knickknack haggling. While in Puerto Vallarta, we actually got some work done too. Dena and I installed more gear, including the new KISS wind generator. I only mention the company because even after using it, talking to other boats, and hearing other wind generators, I still think we got the best one.

And here is one of the great things about cruising: Before you get bored with a place (or a place gets bored with you), you just pull the hook or cast off the lines and move on down the road. After a week in our first cruising destination, we pushed off from the dock and headed back out into a glassy Banderas Bay. With thoughts of adventures to come we cruised down the coast about a hundred miles to a little place called Barra Navidad.

Paradise in paradise

Barra is my favorite place in Mexico. A sleepy little pueblo with cobblestone streets, it is filled with colorful shops and friendly people. It sits on a spit of land that separates the bay from a large lagoon. Along both the bay and lagoon side there are some great little restaurant/palapa bars where good, cheap food and cerveza abound. And so far, it is not overrun by tourists.

I must confess that the little town of Barra is not the only thing I like about the bay. Separated from Barra by a little rio is the super-plush hotel/marina called the Bahia Grande. Its Spanish-style buildings and grounds cover the hillside. A few years before, I had spent a month at the Bahia on a large motor-yacht that I was running, while the owners flew home for

Christmas. I remembered seeing the hotel staff scraping the growth off the dock pilings. They don't even do that at home. It was the cleanest marina I had ever seen. I am not a big fan of marinas for anything but watering and ease of provisioning. They can be hot and dusty, but mostly, they simply cut too deeply into the beverage budget. But this place was something special and I wanted Dena to experience it.

We pulled into the marina under the cover of darkness. Being post season, the marina had only a few boats and most of them were unoccupied, just being stored for the summer. We glided up to one of the empty slips and tied up. A guard came out and welcomed us. He assured us that security was tops. I was not worried.

We got cleaned up at the dock showers and I took Dena on a little tour. For me, the best thing about the place is the pool. It dominates three levels of the grounds. How do you get from one level to the next, you ask? Well, water slides of course! Everywhere there are shady places where you can grab a lounge chair and get some reading/writing done. We raided the ice machine and went to bed early.

We got up with the sun, as we had a full day ahead of us. Normally, you would want to head straight to the local authorities and check in. At $1.70/foot per night I could only afford one day at the Bahia Grande, so checking in would have to be postponed while our full schedule of playing and relaxing would commence immediately. We spent the day reading, writing, swimming, sliding, playing pool volleyball, and hanging with Mexican millionaires at the swim-up bar. Late that afternoon, I set up the light stern anchor and nylon rode at the bow (the all chain rode hadn't been run yet), and we motored into the lagoon and anchored LOW KEY for the first time.

The next day we checked in. Barra has no bank, so to pay our check-in fee we had to take a bus to the next town, Melaque. Of course, we would have to take the bus to Melaque again to check out. But that would not matter because we would have to go to Melaque anyway to catch the bus for the two-hour ride into Manzanillo, to visit Immigration, to get our check-out-of-Mexico paper that we would need to check into the next country we would go to. The Port Captain in Barra forgot to put his stamp on our check-out paper, so we would have to bus into Manzanillo a second time. Of course, we made the most of it.

Where's the boat?

When we got back to Barra that first day, we got right to exploring. There were many fond memories to be dug up. That afternoon, as we made our way through the waterfront restaurant to get back to our dinghy MOTU, we were stopped by a local fisherman type. He was telling me in Spanish that our boat had "gone off." He did not mean the dinghy. A lot of things ran through my mind, disturbing my cherished state of inner peace. The wind was up, could we have dragged? Fortunately, the tide would be rising for the next few hours and we were anchored in a nearly enclosed lagoon with a sandy bottom. How bad could it be?

The man asked if he could help us. I paused and looked him over. Could he have had something to do with our sudden unfortunate situation? I thanked him and told him no. We puttered out with our 2-hp dinghy at two knots. It was going to be a very long trip. We had parked LOW KEY in the lagoon about a mile away. If she really had dragged, she would be another half mile away.

We rounded the point to see the empty space where our home had been anchored. I felt sick. A minute later we could see the speck, which was LOW KEY, at the other end of the lagoon, cocked to one side, trying to get ashore.

Our new friend pulled along side with his *panga* (a long, narrow, open fiberglass boat with high prow and a big outboard), and he offered his help to us again. I had gotten boats off the bottom before. With the rising tide, all we really had to do was reset the anchor with the dinghy and the boat would eventually float free. I thought about the consequences of allowing this guy to help us, including the inevitable demand for a gargantuan fee. But something told me to give this guy a shot.

We climbed on board the panga and tied little MOTU astern. We shot off at 30 knots across the lagoon. As we coasted up to LOW KEY, I stood at the bow and called out to her, "Where do you think you're goin'? There's nothing to see over here." My little boat had gotten herself into quite a predicament. The wind was howling to forty knots on that end. The wind generator sounded like a small prop plane preparing for take off. She was clearly aground, leaning away from the blow. The bow had somehow turned downwind away from the anchor. Mini swells were hitting the stern and splashing up, salting the cockpit and the inside of the dodger. She had her nylon anchor rode clinched tightly in her teeth. From the bow, the rode strained aft along her hull disappearing into the churning muddy water at her stern.

I hopped aboard, lashed the wind generator and made my way forward. The anchor rode was clearly still attached to the anchor. This was not a case of foul play. I threw our Mexican friend a line and he tied it to the stern of the panga.

There was a lot going on. I had my hands full, keeping lines out of the panga prop while Roberto whipped the panga around to turn it back into the wind. Through the din of the howling wind I suddenly heard a second outboard motor, loud and very close by. I looked over and saw Dena hanging over the rail. She was half in the panga and half in our little dinghy. It seems that the 2-hp engine had tilted itself back down into the water at some point. The dinghy being towed through the water had turned the prop fast enough to bump start the engine. In an effort to climb back into the safety of the dink, the little engine ripped its own mounting bracket off. With my hands full of recovery lines I could only stand there and watch in awe. Like a mini crocodile wrestler, Dena tackled and rolled around with the live engine as it revved and flailed about on the hard dinghy floor. She finally got it shut down and pulled herself back into the panga. We towed LOW KEY back across the bay and reset her, this time with her all chain rode and heavier CQR. I had used the light stern gear before because I hadn't taken the time to assemble her heavier gear. In the shifting winds the light rope rode had swung around and picked up the anchor. We had all worked together to complete our important mission and shared the pride of a job well done.

With our batteries topped up and our refer iced down (and our boat saved), I invited our new friend aboard for a frosty Pacifico. He accepted. His name was Roberto. I thanked him. He was a mess. Like his formerly clean panga, he was covered in mud and brackish water, and I felt kind of bad. Over our second beer, I offered him some cash for his time and effort and he accepted without a higher counter offer. Even more compelling, he said that he would return the next day to clean our boat bottom for free. He did as he said and from then on whenever he would see us waiting for a water taxi, he would insist that we ride with him. Before we left Barra, he gave Dena a very cool little bracelet. If you make it down Barra-way, keep an eye out for our friend Roberto and his panga DORARIA, and be sure to say hola for us if you see him.

Twice now, cruisers have told us that it took a couple months before they had their first "cruising moment": the morning, the afternoon, the evening when their initial cruiser fears and frustrations had dwindled enough so they could finally realize that this was their life and how lucky they were to be living it. As we waded through those early cruising waters which for us had been a state of constant tuning, gear installation and long sails (now coupled with a semi-perilous dragging event), I had wondered when that moment would come for us. That evening I looked around me. The boat was coming alive with systems. The wind generator was whooshing, the refer was thrumming, pumps were a-pumping, and a day's worth of challenge lay behind us—slain. That night, we sat calmly at anchor off the coolest little town in Mexico. We were out in the cockpit, snug in our beanbags, stars blazing above with cold Pacificos and a warm breeze to keep us company. I felt a powerful sense of well-being and wondered if this was what they were talking about.

CHAPTER 2

Twenty-Seven Days at Sea

We fueled up, departed Barra Navidad, Mexico, and headed for the Galápagos Islands, 1,400 miles to the southwest. Officially, hurricane season was to start in Mexico in a week but hurricanes do not always follow a strict schedule and have been known to occur much earlier. We started out heading due south to get to the relative safety of the generally agreed upon southern boundary of the hurricane belt—10 degrees north latitude. We sailed as much as we could, but fired the engine for the calms and when the wind was on the nose. Our SSB (long range radio) was still in a box so the only weather info we got, on two occasions, was from other ships that were passing by. I have heard hardcore singlehanders say, "What good is knowing bad weather is coming? All it gives you is more time to worry."

We had to motor more than I had expected. By the time we were closing on 10° north, I could tell we would not have enough fuel to make it through the last couple hundred miles of expected calms near the Galápagos. We talked about turning right instead. The southeast trades were just a few degrees away. They should be able to take us the 2,500 miles to the legendary Marquesas. Dena was flexible (she did yoga) and she thought we had enough food. I knew we could make the fresh water last. We turned right.

The weather was a little unsettled just north of the equator with variable winds, some rain, and some lightning. For some protection from a lightning strike I implemented my own version of the Bitchin anti-lightning device. I wrapped the end of a ten-foot piece of anchor chain around the backstay and dropped the rest over the transom. The concept being that you give the strike a clear path to the water so it doesn't try to blow its way through the boat. I don't know if it works, but it made me feel better.

Between squalls we encountered a large flock of blue-footed boobies, widely renowned as the goofiest seabirds. You will find them in the most remote stretches of the ocean. Twice, I have had a booby catch himself on a fishing lure that we were towing. The next day the flock returned. On the third day, one of the birds landed on the stern. There he stayed for 20 hours. We named him Boob, of course. Every time I had to go aft to mess with Nessie the windpilot, Boob would take a swipe at me with his beak. You could say we didn't get along all that well. Still, towards the end I was getting worried about him. He must have been sucking up too much of the exhaust fumes because he was starting to look a little woozy. He finally fell off into the water. He managed to get airborne again and came back and landed in front of the dodger. After a couple of hours of fresh air he took off, never to be seen again.

He left the boat near Clipperton Island. An interesting thing about Clipperton, aside from its very cool past, the large atoll did not show up on our Garmin electronic chart. I even paid for the extra chart CD. I only noticed it when I checked the paper chart. It was a good lesson for me to learn before arriving at areas with even more challenging navigational environments.

Adversity strikes

We have all heard those sacred words, "reef early and often," and they are words to live by. In the yacht delivery business we have another saying that goes, "reef for comfort." If the boat is heeling excessively, then reef. It makes for faster, more fun, safer sailing. But on the hard beat en route to the trades, I was reminded of the #1 reason for reefing—preventing expensive sail failure.

It was before sunrise and still pitch dark. The wind was coming from right where we needed to go. We were motorsailing with just the main up, as close to the wind as we could go without luffing the main. Sheeted in hard at the centerline, the main reduces rolling while providing some lift to weather. It is the fastest, most comfortable way to make the climb to a windward destination. We had 15 to 20 knots of wind and the main was not reefed yet. LOW KEY is not prone to easy heeling which in turn puts even more pressure on a sail. That day I learned that with very old sails, reefing only when heeling excessively can be reefing too late.

LOW KEY was pumping through the waves, efficiently motorsailing upwind. With a bang, the mid part of the main let go and the whole thing started flapping. I remember thinking how the timing was unfortunate. It was coming up on six in the morning. I was a little tired, just coming off watch and though we were just south of 10 north we still did not have much of a cushion. But here we were with no main and a strong headwind pushing us back north. We were losing our hard-fought southing. I looked up and noticed that the tear was below the top reef. I could triple reef the sail which would bring the torn areas out of the wind and we could continue on. I then made a poor decision.

Dena popped out the hatch and took the helm while I proceeded to reef the sail as I normally would. The tear was producing more than the normal reefing procedure flapping and before I could get the sail tightened up, another tear opened up the top of the sail. Oops! I should have pulled the whole sail down and reefed it on the boom then re-hoisted it.

I had a spare main onboard, so I dug it out and proceeded to swap mains. Changing mainsails can be a big job even in a slip. To make things a little more challenging, we were now motoring into a short, steep swell. Without a mainsail up to steady us, LOW KEY was hopping and rolling quite a bit. I will usually turn and sail off the wind while working on deck. On long passages, what's a mile or two lost? The motion is more comfortable and the experience less salty, but we could not afford to lose any southing this time of year.

Finally, the job was done and the new sail (actually I think it was the original mainsail that LOW KEY came with) was up and triple reefed, sheeted in hard, and we were on our way—for 15 minutes. Bang, mainsail #2 let go. The material was just too old for that kind of use. I lashed it to the boom and put up the small, heavy headsail (the #2) and contemplated lying down for a bit. To make my rest even more worry free I decided not to take any chances with our last heavy-weather sail. Through a tired haze I went forward once again to lower the #2, reef it, and pull it back up. When it was done we set up Nessie to steer the boat and shut down the engine. The only way we could make any southing was on a slow starboard tack heading ESE, away from our tropical destination. That was good enough. We were both exhausted. I turned up the VHF radio, tuned the radar detector, and we both went to sleep.

The next day we went to work on repairing mainsail #1. It was Dena's idea. I was still too burnt to contemplate such a grand undertaking. It was in three pieces, but with just two of the tears sewn up we would be able to sail single-reefed. It worked beautifully. The boat shot back up to windward, pointing much higher than with headsail alone. Note to self: Never underestimate a woman with a needle and thread. We tacked over and were then laying our Marquesas Islands destination.

Smooth sailing

We mostly had good wind after that, all the way to the equator where Dena graduated from pollywog status to become a *shellback*. It is an old tradition when sailors make their first crossing of the equator that they be initiated, I mean welcomed into, the Order of Shellback by Neptune himself (or someone impersonating the Roman god of the sea). After our impromptu ceremony, we partook of some good Caribbean rum given to us as a parting gift.

Then the strangest thing happened. We both passed out just before the equator. I awoke on the other side of the much celebrated line, to the sound of a large slow-turning motor close by. It was a 100-foot Chinese fishing boat passing safely abeam of us, a thousand miles from anywhere. What were the odds? The radar detector had not detected it, probably because the Sanford and Son-built fishing boats don't have radar. The tiller was still in my hand, the autopilot disengaged. I had wanted to hand steer across the equator. I looked at the GPS and saw that we had crossed on a perfectly straight course. Was I so skilled that I could steer in my sleep? It seemed unlikely. Had Neptune himself, appreciative of our honors to him, guided us across? I like to think so.

South of the equator was a much happier place for me. We were far from the threat of the bigger tropical depressions and well on our way to my favorite islands. And then, we were becalmed. With 1,274 miles to go, there was no use in motoring. We were in the middle of the tradewind belt, but we were completely stopped. Without any sailing to do, I was bored. I do not know how long he had been there, but we noticed that there was a five-foot shark just ambling along in our ½-knot wake, there to feast on the bounty that our shadow lured. That night we really checked out the stars. It was amazing.

And when you are becalmed for a day or two and the wind comes back up, you really appreciate it. The wind would be off and on for the rest of our sail to the Marquesas. Miniature dolphins came to visit three evenings in a row, right around sunset. They would come flying up and Dena would go to the bow to talk and sing to them as they played in the wake. On their third and last visit, by accident or by plan, they scared up a bunch of flying fish and sent them soaring up into Dena. The dolphins and I had a good laugh while Dena tried to get the slime and scales off. A couple of minutes later the dolphins all disappeared. The next thing we saw were very large tuna jumping out of the water all around the boat. I was hoping one would accidentally land in the cockpit saving me the trouble of getting the fishing rigs out. Then I saw the pools of blood. I had never thought about it but of course, dolphins are a vicious predator—a predator that, for some reason, chooses to be nice to humans.

Then there were the nights with the full moon. It was like soft daylight in the middle of the ocean. About four days out from our destination, for two nights in a row we saw a large ship. It was all lit up and just seemed to be doing giant slow circles and ignoring our radio calls. It was not towing trawls and it seemed too large to be a research boat. It was probably one of those huge fish processing plants that you hear about.

The day before our arrival we heard a large bump from the front of the boat. It was a full five-gallon diesel container just floating off the islands, and I wanted it. I looked around the boat, at the poled-out whomper (a large genoa sail) and the vanged-out main, and decided I would let it go. It would end up drifting ashore eventually, a nice gift for some islander.

On our last day, both support cables for the large spinnaker pole broke in separate bouts of failure. I was glad that they had waited until they got us where we were going. That's how you know your boat likes you (or that you've been lapse in your inspections).

And then, Land Ho! After 27 days and over 3,300 nautical miles, there was Ua Huka off the port bow. Surprising as it always is, that little box of solder and silicone really did know where it was, even after weeks at sea. It was a feast for the eyes, all of that lush green on sharp peaks. The decision had to be made. Do we slow down and enter in the morning light, or do we continue to plow along in a perfect wind and enter the anchorage at midnight? The chart showed the entrance to Taiohae Bay on the island of Nuka Hiva to be wide and well lit. We go in tonight.

As we turned toward the entrance to the bay, I went to the bow to douse the big headsail for the last time. It was pitch black out and all I could see were the shore lights deep in the bay. I looked over the side and under the glow of the green navigation light was the back of the biggest dolphin I had ever seen. And then there were three. They were swimming along with us, turning from red to green as they crossed the bow—our welcoming party for our hard-won island paradise.

CHAPTER 3

Arrival in Paradise

Dena got up early. She went on deck to have a look around. We had anchored, late the night before, in the volcanic crater that makes up Baie Taiohae in the Marquesas Islands. During our twenty-seven-day crossing, I had bored her with my stories of this place with its spectacular scenery and rush of earthy fragrance. Twenty-seven days of watches—three hours on, three hours off—and I was ready for my first sleep-in since Mexico. It was not to be. For half an hour, she hopped around the deck exclaiming things like, "Look how green this place is" and "Check out those peaks" and "I can smell the flowers from here" and on and on. It was nice to see that someone else appreciated what no words can describe.

I put the dinghy in the water. We motored right up to a likely victim . . . er, cruising boat and said hello. Dena mumbled to me, "What are you doing?" I told her, "This is what you do!" It was Dan and Sandra on a boat called MARIPOSA. Although they were complete strangers, it was like we were old friends. They asked about our crossing and gave us all of the important local info on things like checking in and where to get the CBT, as well as the very important directions to the nearest boulangerie for our first fresh French baguette—the bread that would be a staple for us while cruising the French Polynesian Empire.

We had arrived on a good day. It was the "schools letting out for summer" festival. As tribal drum beats echoed across the bay, we made our way ashore. We dinghied in through some small surf and tied to a tree. We followed the music and found a mini outdoor arena set up around the town meeting area by the beach. All of the younger school children of the island had come to Taiohae in their full dress costumes to perform their dancing shows. There were five groups of 30 or more. After the kids were done, there was an older group that did their much-more-practiced dancing. That was especially cool. It had been years since I had seen any Polynesian dancing and now I was looking forward to finding more as we continued down the "coconut milk run."

We learned that there was another festival coming on the main island of Tahiti. Every four years they invite all of the islands to send their best dancers and their grand dance productions over to compete. That event was being held this year, in the following month. And so for the five days we were there, the Nuka Hiva dancers practiced at the quay directly ashore. Every night, the drums started up after dark. A couple of nights we went in and watched. The other nights we sat on deck and just enjoyed the sounds.

We were out of fresh water and needed to head over to the island of Ua Pou to fill up. Our friends on MARIPOSA bribed us with a couple gallons of watermaker water to first sail over to the next bay and do the waterfall hike with them. Oh, O.K!

I have been to places where you had to hike five miles to see some speck of a ruin that is hardly recognizable. The Marquesas Islands are not like that. Thousands of years old, their tiki-looking statues saturate the coastal villages. They are part of the landscape. I caught myself using the head of one of the little guys as a coaster. You just become used to having them around. Our hike was loaded with them. Dan and Sandra knew some of the valley lore. Ancient Marquesans only ventured inland for one reason, for tribal ceremony. As we hiked and they told their tales, I found myself imagining the life of an ancient Marquesan islander.

It was the end of the hike that brought the big payoff. The last mile or so, we walked a narrow curving path between two towering black-rock cliffs. You could hear the powerful sounds of the planet's third tallest waterfall growing louder. At the end of the trail was a big pool of water. Once there you have to swim across then negotiate a pile of boulders to enter into the inner pool and experience the bottom of the falls. The place had good energy. It made me want to have our own tribal ceremony.

We're sinking

While at the island of Nuka Hiva, I noticed a small leak in the aft bulkhead. It was coming from the direction of the rudder post, but there was no way of figuring out for sure without hauling the boat. Perfect, I thought, the boat needed some bottom paint anyway. The only problem was that the nearest haul-out facility was over 700nm (nautical miles) away. For better or for worse, this accelerated our schedule a bit. When people would ask how we were doing, we would tell them that we were sinking.

We did finally make it over to the island of Ua Pou where we tied up at the pier to steal, I mean take, some water. The Port Captain pulled up in his Land Cruiser and walked over to me. He was a serious looking man. Of course everyone in the islands seems to have that look when you first meet them. I explained that we had only pulled up to the pier to get water and we would be anchoring and coming in to see him shortly. He smiled. He just wanted us to know that the ARANUI, the giant supply ship, was pulling in early in the morning. Cool, I thought.

I had heard a lot about the famous ARANUI. This one was the ARANUI VI. I had read somewhere that the early supply boats were big schooners. In addition to island supplies, they also carried passengers. Some clever passenger, or was it some clever captain, had figured out that, for a price, one could stay on board and see the whole set of islands, venturing ashore for a bit at each one. This new and improved ARANUI had two big cranes over a huge center cargo area with a giant opening hold. The ship also had cruise ship-like rooms for passengers. That could be an interesting way to get a quality look at the Marquesas.

The next day, the ARANUI showed up. It seemed to take up

the whole bay, but somehow it was able to drop an anchor and slide past the little anchored cruisers up to the cement pier. Dena and I had set up our camping chairs on deck. You know the ones. They are canvas with arms that have holders for your cold drink and they fold up and drop into a tubular bag. We sat in our chairs with our big Hinanos, the beer of French Polynesia, and watched the show. To park, the ARANUI had to swing its stern right across the bow of our friends' boat, HRAI ROO. HRAI ROO is a twenty-foot Flicka, a sturdy little toy cruiser with the lines of a traditional East Coast cutter. The ARANUI had line tender boats that were twenty-five feet. The contrast of the boats was comical. And then there was the offloading of gear and supplies and passengers. Most of the community turned out to watch. It was a big event.

We were sinking, so we did not stay long in Ua Pou. We headed out of the bay and made a feeble attempt at sailing to Fatu Hiva. We had heard that you could trade stuff for carvings in Fatu Hiva. We had tons of extra junk, I mean, stuff. The wind and seas were up and the idea of bashing into them for four days did not seem, well, seaman-like in our current state. We turned right (read: downwind and with the swell) and headed for the Tuamotus.

A tip for those who will be headed this way. The French are lightening up. They are allowing boats to pull into the windward island of Fatu Hiva before checking into Hiva Oa or Nuka Hiva (you have to love a place with island names like those). Do not stay too long. Also, as two German boats learned, do not pull anchor and try to sneak out when the customs boat comes into the bay. You could get fined. Be respectful. Smile, even when receiving bad news. It will take you a long way when working with port officials in the countries I have been to.

We finally had a good strong sailing wind. It was a contrast from our strange 27-day crossing from Mexico to the Marquesas with mostly light to no wind. Now that we were island hopping, there was tons of it. Nessie was able to do the driving. We had the Franken-main up, with its big ugly stitched areas, a reminder of two of the longer days of our adventure. The whomper, an oversized genoa, was pulling from the bow. The KISS wind generator was cranking out the amps so we had music and cold sunset beers.

I did have to run the engine once on this passage. It seemed like there was a bit more movement from the beast than usual. When I shut it down, I looked around and found two bolts on the floor of the ER. As it was when finding a stray cotter key on deck, a little alarm went off in the back of my head. Vibration from the heavy diesel had removed both of the bolts holding one of the aft feet to the engine, leaving our diesel three-legged. Tip: Inspect the gear on your boat often, especially if you are on a micro-budget like us. It is easier to take a couple of minutes and have a quick look around now and then than to have gear needlessly self-destruct from neglect, forcing you to deal with the phone calls, shipping and customs delays that are all part of ordering and importing the widget that ends up being the wrong size. Just a quick look!

We spent my 34th birthday on the passage from Ua Pou to Rangiroa. Dena baked a very interesting looking cake and lowered her culinary standards enough to make one of my favorites—Mac n' Cheese baby! The wind was shifty, so I stayed pretty busy with headsail changes. LOW KEY does not have roller furling. It is not that I am a purist or anything. I like a cold beer and a freshwater shower as much as anyone. Roller furling just wasn't in the budget. We finished our day with a rain-driven shower on deck and a sublime sunset.

Main drag

The next day was the Fourth of July, again spent at sea. We put up the flag and fired a couple of expired flares—low across the water, so as not to attract rescue. Dena made pizza from scratch. And then the wind kicked up a bit and brought with it some squallies. I took down the headsail and fully reefed Franken-main. There was still too much of the old sail exposed to the wind and so we blew out the main for the last time. It is really not normal for a main to tear so easily. Most boats will get their mast wet before the mainsail fails. Ours was just old and sun damaged. We would not hoist a mainsail again for over a month. We wouldn't need to.

So the tough little #2 went up at the bow and we sailed through the night, fast and smooth. In the morning, we were on a beam reach in close to thirty knots. I reefed the little headsail mostly to protect it, but also to slow us down so we did not arrive too early.

Nine miles from the entrance to Rangiroa and we still could not make out the island. Rangiroa is one of the Tuamotus and is a low-lying atoll. The first thing we saw were tiny tops of palm trees and the white tower near the entrance. And then a rainbow appeared. It started small, but soon stretched into a full half-circle framing the entrance to the pass. It was magical.

I had been a little spoiled being able to punch up tidal information on the GPS. It had no information to offer me here so I called "any vessel in the lagoon at Rangiroa" to get info on when would be a good time to enter the tidal pass. A vessel did respond: a pretty good time to run the pass was now, so we doused the sails, motored through a honking rip-torn pass, and anchored off the real nice, reed-roofed Kia Ora Hotel.

The last couple of days at sea were a little bumpy-rolly. On a beam reach, we had the occasional breaker crash over the port quarter and come aboard for a visit. It was heaven to be anchored in a calm, crystal-blue-water lagoon, just an hour later.

Tiki bars

We went in and said hi to the gendarme, as required, and caught a ride into town. It turns out that we got on Le Truck headed for Le Pearl farm. Whatever, we got a nice tour of the pearl farm and met Midora and Steve. They were born-again Christian honeymooners, fresh off the plane. They were church friends of the driver and her family. We tagged along for a quick tour of town. They dropped us off back at the Kia Ora where the newlyweds happened to be staying. Dena and I snuck away to the bar. We had just come in from the raw energy of a feisty sea and the next thing I know we are kicking back in a couple of fat chairs while some Tahitian cutie serves us drinks and chopped coconut in a five-star, over-the-water tiki bar. Works for me.

On our way in to see the local dancing at the Kia Ora one night, we stopped by the boat LAST PENNY and met the crew: Mark, Lori, and their young son Mick. Mick was an aspiring writer and one of my seven fans. Mark proceeded to share with us some of his stock from the Caribbean. There was rum from Cuba and beer from Colombia. By the way, we learned that Cartagena has great people, is very safe and incredibly cheap. Still, you do not want to sail along the coast of Colombia, you want to come into Cartagena from sea . . . to avoid the pirates of the Caribbean, of course.

We left Rangiroa with LAST PENNY on a Friday for the overnight to Papeete, Tahiti. They say it's bad luck to leave port on a Friday. I don't know about that, but we did have a squall sweep across the lagoon, out of nowhere, and swallow us up just as we entered the treacherous tidal pass to leave. I would claim that it was my superb seamanship and outstanding navigational ability that saved us from joining the yacht we saw washed up on the beach, but actually, Dena was driving and she just "steered the little triangle on the GPS" and lead us out safely.

We pulled into Papeete at night and parked bow-to at the city quay. In the morning, we found that we were parked amongst the French derelicts and liveaboard boats and fifteen feet from the world's loudest street. We moved over by the other cruisers who were parked at a much more peaceful spot in front of a construction site.

We're having company

Our first guest was flying in in a couple of days. The forward cabin still had boxes in it, so we had a boat-parts give-away on the dock. It consisted of stuff that I had figured out we would not be needing. In the evening, we hung out with our fellow cruisers on their boats along the festive quay.

Our guest Tom arrived. We let him take the first day to get settled in and have a quick look at Papeete. I could tell, though, that he was ready to get right to cruising. The next morning, we motored out the pass at Papeete and put up the whomper. I could see the whitecaps and swells ahead, but I underestimated them. We were leaving the broad lee of the island of Tahiti and were entering the winds that were being shot through the channel between Tahiti and Moorea. The wind built from 10 to 40 knots in 15 minutes. I am the one always telling people that you have plenty of time to reef if you are just paying attention. I cast off the halyard and pulled the big sail onto the deck while Tom steered down the building swells. I got the whomper into a bag and hooked up the #2 and walked back to the mast to hoist it. "We are still doing four knots," yelled Tom over the howling wind. We were sailing with no sails up. We were sailing four knots bare-poled.

I went to hoist the little headsail and could not find my end of the halyard. I had let it go up into the mast where it disappeared. Oops! Did the stopper knot come out? Did I make the knot too small? Did I untie the knot for some reason? Who cares? We were at sea in the biggest winds and seas of the trip so far, we had a guest onboard, and I could not hoist a headsail. Still without a mainsail, I accepted my demotion to power-boater and fired up the engine.

We motored in through the pass at Baie Cook on Moorea and anchored in the quiet back bay among very grand volcanic peaks. We cranked up the Buffett and sat back with a cold beer, having survived our own mini storm.

The next day, Tom and I re-ran the halyard. It took a trip to the masthead. I had to take the double sheave out of the top of the mast to fit the end of the halyard back in.

The traveling circus was in town, so we dinghied in that night to see it. On this tiny island, in this little bay, was a mini-circus with bumper cars, tiny rides, and booths with circus games. This little eight-year-old local girl chased Tom around all night trying to get him to take her on the bumper cars. The Moorean dance troupe did their show and it was very good. We finally retired to our friend's boat LAST PENNY for a couple of rum chasers.

While visiting the next bay over, we joined with some other cruisers and hiked up the interior of Moorea. We started out on roads and then switched to a deep jungle trail that climbed high into the ridge. Along the trail we encountered rock foundations from ancient ceremonial buildings. I was craving an ice cream and not a minute later, we rounded a corner in the trail and found ourselves in a small parking lot among buses, jeeps, and a concession stand that had ice cream. This was a popular tourist spot apparently. There was a nice observation deck built there that looked out over both bays.

Before we left Moorea, we took the dinghy on an expedition to find the friendly stingrays. There was a bungalow hotel that drew the stingrays by feeding them everyday. We pulled up just as a boat full of hotel guests was leaving. The driver tossed us a spare fish head. It was the size of a basketball. We slipped into the water and began to feed the rays. They started getting really friendly. I pulled myself back into the dinghy to snap some pictures. The water was about four feet deep and crystal clear. Tom and the girls were getting mobbed by the rays. It was pretty funny.

From the dinghy I could see the black tip reef sharks circling around the perimeter. They were waiting for the humans to go so they could steal the big fish head. I got back into the water. I liberated the fish head from our crew and swam it over to the sharks, tossing it into the mix. Dena tried to swim in and get it, but it was too late. I grabbed her by the ankle and pulled her back. A shark rushed in and bit hard into the fish head. I was surprised to hear a resounding underwater crunch. Then another came in and took a bite, thrashing about, trying to rip free a piece of the flesh. Then there were five, then ten, all swimming about excitedly, sometimes coming straight up to us in their deranged feeding state and jerking away at the last second. I had started a feeding frenzy. "Everyone back in the boat," I said calmly, trying to cut my losses. I was already in trouble for stealing the head. Imagine the lashings I'd get if someone lost a triceps.

The wind was howling the whole time Tom was aboard. Twice we sailed out of the bays at Moorea to deliver him back to Tahiti to catch the flight home. Twice the winds beat us back. Without a mainsail to help us point, we were looking at eight or ten hours of hammering into steep fifteen footers. I think Tom would have enjoyed it, but we instead elected to drop him ashore to take the ferry over.

Dancing girls

A few days later, the wind just died and we motored the fifteen miles to Tahiti in a dead calm. Why go back to Papeete? We wanted to see the Heiva Festival, the biggest event in Polynesia. Also, if you check the boat out of French Polynesia at Papeete, you can purchase duty-free fuel at less than half price! (I later learned that you can get the same deal in Bora Bora.)

As soon as we got the hook down on the island of Tahiti, Jim and Debbie on their little cutter HRAI ROO told us about a wreck dive nearby. We all dinghied out in front of the airport. From the dinghy you could see, in thirty feet of beautiful clear blue water, a little piper cub airplane next to the empty hull of a small, full-keel sailboat. Somehow, it made me very uncomfortable seeing them at the bottom of the sea like that. I swam down and tried to sit in the cockpit of the plane but was stopped by a very territorial little brown fish. At first I thought that he had bumped into my mask by accident. The second time, I knew he was serious.

The next day, we took Le Truck into town to see some of the Heiva events. I returned to LOW KEY around lunch time to check the bilge, still sinking you know, only to find my dinghy not the way I had left it. On the end of the dock and all over my dinghy were topless vahines (Tahitian babes). No kidding. They were just trying to get some sun. They apologized and moved off the dinghy onto the pier without incident. I did finally make it back to town to meet up with everyone and see the incredible Polynesian dance competition. Amid tiki flames and reed covered props, large dance groups of thirty or more locals showed off their beautiful island dress and passionate dancing skills. Each routine lasted an hour or more.

Work?!!

Alas, it was time to leave Tahiti. Dena and I fueled up and had a perfect, light air sail back to Moorea, followed by a nice overnighter getting to watch the sun rise over Huahine as we sailed into Raiatea. I heard our friends from LAST PENNY on the radio. I called them. They were in a marina that was only eight dollars a night! They saved us a spot. Turns out that the marina was owned by the people that were supposed to haul us out of the water. Perrrfect.

We hauled two days later. Then the work began. As you know, boatyards charge you by the day so from the time they pull you out to the time they splash you, you work all the hours that you can stand. We were in the yard for seven days. LOW KEY never had a problem with blisters before but the warm water had brought them out along the waterline and elsewhere. We ground out the moisture and filled them with underwater epoxy. After sanding, we covered the work with underwater, two-part paint. They finally put us back into the water and we crawled back to the dock. We were burnt.

It was good to have access to a water spigot so we could wash the yard scum off the boat. And, it was good to not be sinking anymore. That first night we had a guest. We were watching a movie and I heard a noise. It wasn't a boat noise. I poked my head out the hatch and a form brushed past me. It was very dark out and I had been looking at the TV, so I could see nothing. I heard him ride off on a bike. Normally, I would not think much of it, but a couple days before I had my shoes stolen from the dock. They were not exactly shoes, they were flip flops, but they were my favorites and I had not quite gotten over the loss. "There is no chance he'll be back," I told Dena.

Later that night, I was writing on the laptop in the saloon. Dena screamed from the forward stateroom. The next thing I knew, I was sprinting through the boatyard close behind our visitor. The computer screen was not as bright as the TV, I could see him well, on his bike, just out of reach. He pulled away and I slowed and then stopped, inviting him to come back, if just for a minute. Dena said she could hear me yelling at him from back at the dock. He did not come back.

Though I think that our visitor was simply a curious local, during our visit to Raiatea there were a few thefts from boaters. Things like surfboards and dive gear from the decks of anchored vessels. I suspect it was the work of one or two bad apples. We felt safe in all parts of Raiatea that we visited at all times.

The islands of Tahaa and Raiatea are two connected atolls that form what looks like a figure 8. Waiting for the new mainsail to come we used our spare time exploring Tahaa for over a week. It was great. We anchored off the *motus*, the outer reef islands, where the water is always crystal and the sand is always white powder. It seemed like we had, until now, been in a hurry to get to the next place. First it was to stay ahead of hurricane season, and then it was to get to a place we could haul out to find our little leak. But now we had to stop. We were forced to enjoy this piece of paradise.

While at the island of Tahaa in Apu Bay, we celebrated Dena's birthday. Steve and Jeri on SUNJAMR helped me out. I had arranged to meet a different boat at Tahaa. That boat was supposed to help me surprise Dena. That boat was nowhere to be found. SUNJAMR came through, offering to host an impromptu party and even bake a cake. We were back in business. We had a great evening with Steve and Jeri and their guests, Anna and her Welsh bartender, Neil.

A new sail

We did finally return to the yard to pick up our new sail! The boatyard had explained that we should use an expediter to clear customs. It wasn't a good idea. We didn't get the sail any faster and it was expensive. Leaving Raiatea, the island of thieves, we had to say goodbye to our friends on MINTAKA. They were flying home to go back to work for six months. They were putting their boat up in the yard while they were gone. "Work," I pondered. What could that be about?

Bora Bora. I had been taunted by its silhouette for almost a month now. Nearly everywhere we went around Raiatea and Tahaa, we could see its epic outline on the horizon. The image that had haunted me as a kid taunted me now. Here I was returning (for the third time) but this time was different. I was returning to explore the island on my own boat—following the dream that changed my life.

CHAPTER 4

Bora Bora and Beyond

Our new mainsail had finally arrived. We had spent a month sailing the sister islands of Raiatea and Tahaa, waiting for the sail to arrive from China. Even in those amazing islands, that was too long. Too much time in one place would mean less time in another. Bora Bora sat idyllically on the horizon taunting us at each sundowner. And finally we sailed out the pass on the west side of Tahaa, close astern of our friends on the ketch DAWNSBELLE. In light air we crossed the channel and moved into the lee of legendary Bora Bora. We maneuvered in through the pass and took moorings at the Bora Bora Yacht Club. Having cheated death yet again, we settled into our deck chairs with our arrival coldies, just in time to witness the end-all of spectacular sunsets.

The next morning we took the dinghy into the BBYC dock and met the owner. Try as we might, we could not coax a beverage from him. "We are closed early this season," he said. "There were not many boats this year." He did, however, provide me with a memorable quote. Sammy, the hot babe from DAWNSBELLE, asked him, "Are you French?" There was an uncomfortable silence. It seemed like a fair question. He was running a business in French Polynesia and he had an accent, Belgian if I had to guess.

He finally exclaimed, "French! If I were French I would have to kill myself! Only I wouldn't have the guts." I think that even my French friends would agree . . . that's pretty funny.

We sailed off the mooring and tacked up the lagoon, trying out the new mainsail. It was great to be able to point high into the wind again. We tacked past town and up the bay to the renowned Bloody Mary's, sailing up to a mooring out front. Most of the inner lagoons at Bora Bora are 70–90 feet deep. I ain't anchorin' in that. We went into the bar for an icy Hinano from the tap. I had brought a *Latitudes & Attitudes* burgee for owners Craig and Richard who were friends of the magazine. They were nowhere to be found. Bloody Mary's has the most beautiful dock. If you eat in their amazing restaurant, you can spend the night at a mooring out front and even pull up to the dock and take good water.

We did finally find a shallow spot to anchor on the west side of Bora Bora. On the south end of Motu Toopua there is an over-the-water bungalow hotel called the Bora Nui, a Sheraton Hotel. We parked across the lagoon in twenty feet of clear, turquoise water over soft white sand. At night, by the light of the moon, you could see the boat's shadow on the floor of the lagoon. There was a good snorkel reef nearby and a nice breeze all of the time. It was perfect. There must have been twenty cruising boats anchored there. It was great to hang out with our cruising friends, both old and new. It seemed like every night we were having sundowners aboard a different boat.

A couple days into our wonderful stay in the anchorage, the Sheraton sent a little bald Frenchman out in a skiff to tell all of the boats to leave the area. He said that the hotel owned the water and that the Coast Guard would be by in the morning to check our papers. I was pretty sure Napoleon was yanking our anchor chains, but like most of the cruising boats there, I could not risk a fine. Most had expired visas, or like us, had already checked out of the country, so we all turned tail and moved up the road (we found an even better spot near the north end of the motu). One boat called INTEGRITY (of course) had their papers in order and stayed in defiance. The next day the Coast Guard did not come, and there were no repercussions, just some bad feelings toward Sheraton.

The more avid (or is it rabid) reader of *Latitudes & Atti-*

tudes may remember the great beer caper of Share the Sail—
Tahiti 2001. It was in that same bay that we parked LOW KEY
now, revisiting fond memories. At first we had the whole pris-
tine bay to ourselves. The other cruising boats had all sailed
over to the mainland to try and anchor in the deep gorge anchorage by Bloody Mary's. It took a couple windy nights, with
some daytime radio taunts from LOW KEY about how good we
had it, for the rest of our cruising friends to move over to our
little paradise.

A large sailing yacht pulled in. I used to skipper yachts. I
knew that when the owner left it was time to relax. I had been
keeping an eye on the boat and crew and noticed that the owner
was not aboard (owners of yachts must return home to make
money so that we as crew can continue cruising paradise in the
style we're accustomed to). I took the dinghy over to say hello.
Mitch and Tim were moving the boat to Hawaii and stopped
off in Tahiti for a look see. They invited us over for a sundowner. The next day I cleared my afternoon schedule (ha!) to
help Tim. He needed someone to drive the tender (read: large,
center-console dinghy with an inboard engine) while he wake-
boarded. He invited Dena as well and we ripped it up. The next
day we motored over to our friends on MERMAID (owner Robin
is now our ad girl at the *Latitudes & Attitudes* main office) and
picked up young Stacy to come take some turns with us. Fun
was had by all.

Good news! While I was working on LOW KEY, Dena motored over to the main town of Vaitape with the little 20-foot
cruiser, HRAI ROO. A group of charter boaters from San Francisco's *Latitude 38* took a picture of little ROO with Dena as
crew. They told her that she was going to be in a magazine.

On our last day in Bora Bora we sailed back over to Bloody
Mary's to say goodbye, and to get some water. Rick was there
that time and thanked me for the burgee and said to say hi to
Bob. We convinced him to sit down and drink beers with us for
a couple of hours. It wasn't difficult. As we were leaving he asked
us to come back after closing for a party. Party? Us? Well, O.K.

It was a party that they were throwing for the international crew of a big cruise ship parked in the bay. Not a finer group of people have I ever met (outside the cruising community, of course). Dena and I sat at the end of the bar as the party grew. We started to talk to some of them and by the end of the night the party was at our end of the bar. We wanted to know about cruise ship life and they wanted to know about our travels on the smaller boat. Dena kept getting dragged off to lambada by this beautiful Italian girl. I wasn't sure what would come of it, but I figured if I played my cards right . . .

At 0930 we cast off from the mooring ball in front of Bloody Mary's, our home away from home. As we sailed away I noticed a small French Navy tender pulling up to one of the other moored boats—bullet dodged. We were still within our 90-day visa limit, but I had checked out of the country at Papeete so I could get duty-free fuel. As I sailed by the large French Navy ship I got on the radio to warn a couple of other cruisers that were still in the area. To keep myself out of trouble I used a code name instead of LOW KEY. Just after switching back, a loud, super-clear, accented voice called us on Channel 16. It was obviously from the high-watt radio of the Navy ship. I was busted.

"LOW KEY, LOW KEY, LOW KEY, this is the TAHITIAN PRINCESS, TAHITIAN PRINCESS, on 16." It turned out to be the doctor of the cruise ship who had spotted us sailing by and had commandeered the VHF in the wheelhouse. He called to thank us for being at their party. We thanked him back and slipped out the pass, leaving Bora Bora and more good memories astern.

Between Bora Bora and Suvarov we encountered a little weather. The wind had been light and aft all day so I had the whomper up, held out to starboard by the spinnaker pole. The whomper is our largest headsail and when poled-out I almost do not miss the fact we are out of spinnakers.

After dark, the wind built and then built some more. For the off-watch person, we would set up a bunk for sleeping on the lower (downwind) settee in the saloon. It was comfy. As I awoke for my watch, I could hear some ruckus. Somehow though, you do not get the whole picture just from the sounds inside the boat. I came up on deck and saw that hell's fury was upon us. Through blinding rain I strained to see the towering swells rushing at us from aft, raising the stern and making us surf before finally moving under us. Nessie was steering us perfectly down our course, right where I had set her three hours before. The wind pilot gets its strength from the wind, so that night it drove the boat easily.

With the rain clouds blocking out the moon and the starlight, the bow was hard to see. As we accelerated down the next swell, the bow pushed up its spray, and on each side the nav lights painted the flayed water in glowing red and green. From there I looked up and saw the still poled-out whomper and realized that we were a bit over-canvassed. Although things looked dire for us, I try not to make any rash decisions just after waking up.

Dena was there, bundled up in all of her gear. She briefed me like she was supposed to after her watch, "No ships, but the clouds came up from behind us and brought some swell and wind and rain. Good night," and she went to bed. I considered taking the whomper down, but it would have been a big job, especially with the pole up and with the thirty-plus knots of wind. Besides the possibility that I could end up in the water, there was a decent chance that the sail would tear during its take-down flogging routine. It was likely that this was just a front moving through and that we were in the worst of it. By the time my watch had ended, our situation did not seem so desperate, so I decided to leave the sail the way it was. Three hours later, I awoke to the sun coming up. The rain had left, taking some of the wind with it. The wind was down to a more manageable 20 knots. I got the pole and the whomper down and put up the jib and we sailed on.

Suvarov Atoll and American Samoa

A few days later we arrived at our destination, Suvarov Atoll. Suvarov is part of the Cook Islands. It sits pretty far north of its

fellow Cook Islands and therefore is pretty isolated. We motored in through the pass and rounded the main motu to find a
few boats anchored in the calm spot. We parked and savored
our arrival coldy, this time with Dena's pan-made popcorn on
the side. It always strikes me as such a beautiful thing: One moment you are out in the thick of it, working for each mile in big
ocean swells, and the next, you are sitting quietly in flat calm,
clear blue water, securely anchored, watching the easy undula-
tions of palm trees waving from some white sand island nearby.

We took the dinghy in and were greeted by Maki, a little
black attack puppy, there to investigate all newcomers. We
found the caretakers, Papa John and Baker, at their little settle-
ment in the center of the island. They said hi and immediately
invited us to the evening's BBQ, like we had been there for
weeks. We accepted the invitation and explored the island. As
we were heading back to the boat, I watched as Papa John
zipped out to the pass in his little aluminum boat. Fifteen minutes later he returned to the beach. He pulled the boat up the
sand and dragged out his catch from the bow. It was a nice fat
three-foot tuna that he caught at "his spot" in the pass.

The variety of food that night was amazing. There were
about ten people from three boats, and we all had brought in a
dish. By the end of the night, the boat dishes, at best, were half-
eaten. The food Papa John and Baker had made was gone. Papa
John had wrapped the tuna in palm leaves and "baked" it in a
stone oven. Baker made heart of palm fritters which were awesome. There were two or three other island specialties which I
did not recognize, but consumed heartily. These guys were mas-
ters of their domain.

Even though they asked us to stay, we had to finally leave.
The motu itself was not feeling inclined to let us go either. While
swinging around in the anchorage, LOW KEY had wrapped its
chain around some large bits of reef. From the foredeck, I could
clearly see the nice turns the chain made at each dark patch. I
grabbed my mask and fins and jumped in. We were already
dressed for sea, which was undressed, so it didn't require any
change of clothing. While freeing the chain from under the sec-

ond coral piling, a large blacktip reef shark swam by like I was not even there. His indifference concerned me. Why should he worry—this was his world.

We had a fast trip to American Samoa, averaging six knots on a beam reach. We arrived in the evening to the only tenable harbor, the port of Pago Pago (say Pango Pango). We motored by the customs dock which had no space for us. As required, I gave a quick call to the Port Captain on Channel 16. I was glad not to hear back from him. We had arrived after hours, and I did not want to pay overtime charges. We motored over to the other sailboats, deep in the harbor and anchored up, trying to blend in.

American Samoa is known for having all of the products you would find in the States. Everything is subsidized to keep the prices the same as stateside. Some of our foreign cruising friends would bypass American Samoa because they heard about the high entrance fees. Not us, we were USians! We were going to pull in, stock up on goodies from home, and skate on out.

The next morning we dinghied over to the government wharf and checked in with the big local dudes. Everything was run by Samoans there, and Samoans are huge. The Samoans we met were fairly jolly. While the fit and trim Tahitians acted fierce when encountering visitors, my guess is that the Samoans got by on their size alone to intimidate foreign warriors, greeting them with big confident smiles.

We made the rounds to the various officials and were informed at each stop how much our departure would cost. All told, it would be $117 for the privilege of visiting our own American Samoa. That was four times more than any other country we had been to. FYI: Skip AmSam and sail the extra 60 miles to Western Samoa where Samoans live closer to their roots, entry is $6, and booze is duty-free.

Our first day in a new port is usually a check in/shower/get the lay of the land day. With check-in complete, we searched far and wide for a shower. We finally found a little brick facility sitting alone on a beach, outside of town. The inside was covered with graffiti but the water flowed cool and clean. It was perfect.

Across the street was the public library (read: free Internet). We hopped onto one of the wildly painted buses and cruised out to the big American-type warehouse store called Cost U Less, and stocked up. Dena loved American Samoa. I am sure that part of it was the good variety of cheap American food products. I think that also she liked the place because she could talk to everyone. This was the first stop since we left California where all the people spoke English.

There were only a few cruising boats in Pago Pago. At the wharf we met Krys and Walt and their two little dogs on their boat, MANDARA. They have been out cruising for like five years. Krys noticed my *Latitudes & Attitudes* hat. A big fan, she invited us aboard for a quick one and sent us away stumbling. We met Cliff and Karen on ODYSSEY, commodores of the South Seas Cruising Association. *Latitudes & Attitudes* contributor, Mitch Hart, had his boat KOMFY parked in the harbor but we never caught him onboard. My favorite cruiser-hardship story was Gene and his wife on REFLECTIONS who, like so many other boats we have met, were stuck in port waiting for parts. The thing was that the parts they were waiting for were new blades for the blender.

Our stay in Pago Pago was short. We had guests flying in to visit us in Fiji in ten days. It was time to depart. On our way out we motored over to the wharf to try and get water. Taking up the whole space there was a big, shiny power catamaran called MOANA. I pulled alongside. The owner had flown out but the skipper was there. He was great. He welcomed us to tie up. When our hose would not reach to the dock he offered to give us water from his own tanks. We ended up using his hose to reach the dock. Another nice powerboater—it happens!

Filled with anticipation, we motored out into a flat sea and pointed the bow toward Fiji, just seven hundred miles away.

CHAPTER 5

Fun in Fiji

We left American Samoa with almost no wind. We would have waited for wind, but we were on a pretty tight ss-ch-e-du-le (a seldom used, painful word in the cruising vocabulary). Captain Keith and his wife Joanie, old friends from my yacht captaining days, were flying in to join Dena and me for our cruise around the islands of Fiji. To meet up with them we would first need to sail seven hundred miles, transit the deadly reefs and islets of the Fijian Lau Group and make our way around the big island of Viti Levu.

We were making more southing than necessary so we could keep our apparent wind up. We ended up sailing between the northern Tongan islands of Tafahi and Niuatoputapu. In the middle of the channel between them, a pod of whales surfaced very near by. I have only seen whales a couple of times in all of my sea travels. It was amazing to see them so close. Dena was ecstatic.

The sail was going well until we neared the outer islands of Fiji. I could tell that we were going to arrive at those barrier islands in the dead of night. I had picked a wide area between islets that the chart called a "passage" as our path to the safety of the open sea on the other side. I had programmed the GPS to show me all of the shallows in the area. I double checked the info with both the paper and the laptop charts.

There is a game that we play with the sea. I rarely put myself in unsafe situations, but when I do, the sea enjoys compounding my challenge. I don't take it personally, I just think the sea wants to make me a better sailor. A front came through and the wind moved around and picked up. It went from aft to on-the-nose, directly from where we wanted to go. I changed down to a smaller headsail and reefed the main. The wind had pushed up a short choppy sea and the upwind sailing and tacking became a little uncomfortable to those of us who were spoiled by thousands of miles of easy downwind conditions. I made the decision to crack off the wind and head for a much smaller gap in the islands further north. This meant re-plotting and putting in a new set of waypoints in the GPS. With the coming rain, visibility was also decreasing. Needless to say, this would have been a great time to heave-to, which is to park at sea, and wait until morning.

We continued on. It was not so much the schedule anymore. Our friends would understand. It was more the draw of the Suva Yacht Club hamburger and cold beer that kept us pressing on that night. We closed in on the little islands and reefs, just dots on the GPS. I was about to reconsider our course of action when the wind lightened up and the rain and low clouds disappeared. I could now make out the dark masses at various points on the horizon. I placed and named each one to be sure of my course and to confirm the info the GPS was telling me. I finally went to sleep and left Dena to play amongst the dots on the GPS. She safely guided us through.

The next morning I informed Dena that we would be crossing the International Date Line where our longitude would switch from counting up to counting down. Crossing the date line in that direction meant that we would lose an entire day. The good news was that Dena would be lofted to the position of Golden Shellback. The bad news was that the day we lost happened to be Dena's dog Bella's birthday. Dena had left Bella with her friends Paul and Mary back in California. It was more bad news for Dena than for me because, having skipped that day, I would not have to suffer the onboard festivities of a dog's birthday. The feud between Bella and me went way back. The fact that the dog was smarter than me was central to our conflict. I am pretty sure Bella was convinced that I thought her name was, "Get off the bed!"

We pulled into the protected port of Suva and anchored right off downtown. I pulled out the deck chairs and set them up on the foredeck while Dena rustled up a couple of coldies, and we sat together soaking up all the crazy activity. I had read how checking into Fiji could take hours, if not days. I called the harbormaster and he requested that we pull up to the commercial wharf. I was rushed from office to office. Well practiced, I filled out twelve forms in thirty minutes, paying some fees along the way. That has got to be some kind of Suva record. I found out later that the next day was a holiday and the officials were trying to get out early to get a head start on their long weekend—perfect. Though it was not cheap, I had completed both the check-in and check-out paperwork. In Fiji you have to get clearance to move from one area to another.

And finally, we moved across the bay and anchored off the Suva Yacht Club for a celebratory evening of cheap cold brews and sea story swapping with our fellow cruisers. In this case our cohorts were two youngish couples, one from Australia and another from Germany. I ambled up to the old bar to fetch a couple pitchers for our table. The bartender approached. Was it déjà vu? I recognized the old Fijian instantly from a previous visit and then knew what his next words were going to be. His ageless plea echoed in unison with the one he had expressed to me when we had our first encounter seven years before, "Could you please remove your hat?"

"Yes, of course," I answered, smiled and slipped the *Latitudes & Attitudes* cap from my head to the cubby just under the bar. Fiji has proper British roots.

There's something else about clubs all over the world, outside of the States. Yacht clubs are a place for sailors to hang out, visit and learn from each other. Although closed to non-members onshore they are always open to sailors coming in from other countries. It is a difference that leaves yacht clubs in the U.S. lacking. U.S. clubs have more of an exclusionary country club attitude.

We sailed around the main island to the little town of Nadi (say Nandi). Nadi is where the international airport is. We had arranged to meet Keith and Joanie at a beach that I remembered had cool little hostels along the shore. If we were late they would have somewhere to stay. As I was paying out chain I noticed our friends wading knee deep, each with two coldies in hand. How nice is that? That night we four partied "till the wee hours." It was the first time I had awakened in the cockpit—I must have had fun.

We moved the boat around to a little marina called Vuda Point (say Voonda. . . . gettin' the hang of this?). LOW KEY needed fuel and water and her crew wanted proper showers and access to food and beverage shopping. For a little marina, the place had it all. We had arrived on pizza night. Once a week, the beautiful bungalow hotel next door sold cheap pizzas to draw the yachting community into the restaurant. I don't know what the yachting community was doing that night, but the pizza deal did draw out a bunch of rowdy cruisers.

The next day we sailed across to Malololailai and took a mooring at the Musket Cove Resort/Marina/Yacht Club. Marinas and moorings for LOW KEY? Only when guests are aboard. You either hate this place or you love it. I was a fan. Sure, there is a lot going on with tourists and tour boats and small rental catamarans and windsurfers. LOW KEY nearly sank one of the little cats when its driver lost control at full speed and T-boned our blue boat as she lay quietly at her mooring. Still, the place has its charms. This is the site of the Musket Cove Yacht Club. For a couple dollars you get a lifetime membership given only to ocean crossing cruisers. Membership grants you use of the facilities. This includes the holy grail of cruising: access to a real shower. And then there is the pool and the market and phones and a volleyball court and on and on. The locals there field a pretty good volleyball team. All of this in a Gilligan's Island setting.

My favorite part of the resort is the little "One Dollar Bar." Well, it was a "One Dollar Bar" last time I was there. The name has since changed. They now call it the "Three Dollar Bar" (in Fijian money still very cheap). The little outdoor bar sits away from the hustle of the main property, off on a tiny island. You can dinghy there, of course, but the more adventurous resort guests access the bar via the marina floats. The little island boasts free use of its many BBQs, plays good music and is generally a great place for the crews of cruising boats to congregate.

In the morning, Keith took a tour boat and his surfboard out to the legendary surf island of Tavarua. Joanie joined a dive boat to check out some of the underwater scenery. Dena mixed with the rich and famous, basking in the splendor of Fiji island resort life while I, between shore boat duties, went to work installing the SSB (the long-range radio). During one of my short stints ashore I met Noah and Andrea, a twenty-something couple who was sailing across the Pacific on a coastal Catalina 30. And people think I'm crazy. I say good for them!

After leaving our little island paradise, we sailed north and anchored for lunch off a deserted island. We beachcombed in the warm sand with walking sticks, discovered ancient dwellings, established a simple government based on anarchy and hedonism, and set up a form of religion which only pays homage to cold beer which, as legend had it, only existed in a magic cold box onboard the blue floating island resting just offshore. So we had to leave.

We were in the Yasawa Island group now. In order to visit the tribal islands we had to get a special permit from the government. At the permit office we were carefully instructed on how to properly interact with the island tribes. We stopped at an island called Waya. It is the custom when visiting the villages of the outer islands that you offer the chief a portion of yangona, more widely known as kava. It is a root that is ground up, then chewed by virgins who spit the juice into a bowl. It is then imbibed as an intoxicant by tribal elders. It seems to me that with this process you are also going to end up with a bunch of drunk virgins, coincidence?

Nowadays it is ground up, dipped in water and squeezed through cloth or a sock. We went ashore and presented the chief with the yangona. Utilizing the local lingua taught us by the permit office, we asked his permission to hang out in his village. Our gift was accepted, so we broke out the waterproof volleyball and played until dark with the villagers and the backpackers.

Back onboard, it was time for rum and cokes and even my favorite beef jerky sent from home by sweet Marysa in the *Latitudes & Attitudes* office. For ambiance? Our guests also brought us the newest, coolest cruising CD by Travis of Mystery Tramp.

The next evening, one of the locals adopted us and became determined to set up a kava ceremony for us. It was late and getting dark, with bad weather approaching. She took us to a large thatched hut with a woven mat floor. The room was lit by candles. She sent a small village boy in search of a tanoa (large wooden kava bowl). We laid on the mat floor with pillows. With rain now falling harmoniously on the thatch roof and by the light of the candles, she spoke softly describing to us life in her village. It was very cool.

Back onboard, the wind kicked up; twenty, then thirty, then forty knots plus. I made a dumb mistake that night that I would not soon forget. I left the dinghy, with some of its gear onboard, bobbing astern in the building storm. One of the many reasons I love that dinghy is because it is light weight (Apex A-8). Well, as you might have guessed, the big winds and small chop conspired to flip our little friend, dumping its contents and submerging the head of the 2-hp engine. Dena came out to help. My plan was for us to hang over the side of LOW KEY while she lifted the inverted dinghy and I grabbed any gear that tried to float away. She dove in. I guess she figured this was more a time for action than conversation. It was pitch black, the storm was raging, there was a lot of rain and more wind and both boats were being thrown about. Dena was in the middle of it, swimming around and lobbing gear back into the big boat. We lost the gas can and an oar, and I spent the next hours dismantling the engine, rinsing the pieces in fresh water and then spraying them with Water Displacing-40. The little Johnson outboard had never run right anyway; its ability to fail me could not possibly expand.

When the weather cleared up, we said our goodbyes to Waya and sailed off toward Mana Island. Apparently there was good diving at Mana and other stuff that I don't care much about. Somehow, there was a glitch in navigation and we ended up at the wrong island. We pulled up and took a mooring at the upscale raging backpacker Mecca, legendary Beachcomber Island. With yangona in hand, we motored the dinghy ashore and ambled up to the bar. I asked to see the chief. I did not really expect this island to have a real chief. I just thought we might score a couple of drinks for our attempt at humor. The bartender pointed to a large, older man, "in the Hawaiian shirt," seated in the back of the beach bar. I presented the gift to him and said the appropriate words, "yangona ni taranga." He thanked me for the gift, did his little hand clapping ceremony and welcomed us to his island (read: free mooring and use of the facilities).

It was Keith and Joanie's wedding anniversary. We ate with the backpackers and then headed to the bar/entertainment area. Keith and Joanie were getting "tired" so I took them back to the boat where they could be alone (where more bad weather was knocking the boat around, though I don't think they noticed). I returned to the party to find that Dena had pulled up a chair at the kava table. She had also gotten us an invite to the after-hours kava ceremony up in the village.

Our friends' vacation was winding down, so after our visit to Mana we turned toward the main island of Viti Levu and enjoyed a perfect sail to a place called Saweni Beach. Saweni has a little motel where cruisers go to eat dinner, drink beer, watch CNN and swim in the pool. We did all those things before finally having to say our tearful goodbyes. Keith and Joanie left for the airport, leaving Dena, myself and LOW KEY alone again. The boat seemed so big.

There were only five days before the official start of the southern cyclone season. We had about two weeks of sailing to go to reach the safety of the Australian mainland. I was not too worried. The ocean temperature was still in the 70s—relatively chilly—and cyclones don't like that. We stopped once more at the lovely Vuda Point Marina. In one hour, we fueled, filled with water, dumped the trash, took a shower, did a little shopping, called home and, as we motored out the pass, enjoyed some ice cream.

We hoisted the sails and cruised on toward the pass to leave dear Fiji. As we approached the narrow pass, the wind clocked around onto the nose. I reefed down and for a couple of hours we tried to tack out. It wasn't going to happen. Fiji wanted us to stay. Who would argue with a big group of islands like Fiji?

We cracked off the wind and found the nearest shelter, which happened to be a big fat mooring at the Musket Cove Yacht Club. I think both of us were of a similar mindset: We had fired ourselves up for the coming sea battle of two or three days bashing to windward. And suddenly everything had changed. We found ourselves quietly parked and contemplating a deck shower and an evening at the Three Dollar Bar. It was hugely satisfying.

One good thing about our surprise stop was that I did not have to finish the SSB radio installation at sea. We waited for two days for the wind to swing back to normal before having an easy sail out the pass. As a test for the SSB, I tried to contact one of the weather nets. These weather nets are the greatest thing. These old retired dudes, some are ex-cruisers, devote a very large part of their day in their homes downloading weather info and passing it on via SSB to cruisers. Most will plot your course on their charts and give you a personalized prognosis. I bounced a signal off the atmosphere that reached all the way to Russell radio in New Zealand over a thousand miles away. He heard me fine. I suddenly had the ability to listen in on a vast array of weather info, news and entertainment. It was very cool.

We were back at sea for Halloween. It was a very scary night, indeed—it was the night we ran out of beer. Whose fault was it? Who was in charge of beverage provisioning? It would have served no purpose to place blame amongst LOW KEY's devoted crew (especially since it was my turn). We survived the rest of the passage by tapping into our last-resort emergency reserves of my precious Mexican Pacificos.

Nightfall was fast approaching as we neared the entrance to the Havannah Channel at the south end of New Caledonia. Once you enter the Havannah Channel, you must navigate a well-buoyed corridor, about fifty miles, to get to Nouméa. I got the time change wrong when estimating current and arrived an hour earlier than we should have. The current was still rushing out of the channel beating us back. But there was something else. In the black night, the only thing I could see were the range lights—two lights stacked on a hill that you line up to keep to the middle of the channel. Although I was pointed right at them, they were getting further apart. The GPS was telling me that we were off to the right of our intended course, while the depth was showing the ground coming up. I stayed focused and figured out that not only was the current running out, it was pushing us sideways toward the invisible reefs off to starboard. I turned the boat far to port, oddly leaving the range lights off the starboard side. They finally started to drift back together. It was a good lesson.

Exhausted from the last watch, arrival preparations, and surprise navigational challenge, I passed the helm to Dena and went below for some zzzz's. She guided us safely through the islands and turns and buoys. I awoke to her giggling about what a great job she was doing. We had come a long way.

In the early morning light, we pulled into the city wharf at Nouméa. There was time before customs would be up and around, so we snuck up to the showers and waited for someone to open the door. Customs was very friendly, and as it is in other French possessions, the check-in process was painless and free. A lot of cruisers complain about the high cost of food in the French Islands. If you want to partake of the suddenly available high-end cheeses and $11 jars of olives, then yes, French Islands are expensive. But if you eat what the locals eat: rice, pasta and that amazing fresh, morning baguette bread, then the food is very cheap. For the ease of customs alone, I search out French possessions . . . which are everywhere.

We had pulled into Nouméa only to get our Australian six-month visas. The nice lady at the Australian consulate gave us all of the paperwork. Among a lengthy list of tasks required to enter Oz was a mandate to see a doctor and get a chest X-ray. It looked like we were going to be in Nouméa for a few more days and a few more dollars. We were leaving the consulate when I turned and went back to the window and asked if there was another way. We left ten minutes later with a couple of three-month electronic visas.

Six days into the southern cyclone season, we fueled up duty-free and sailed excitedly out the pass. We were finally on our way to finish our Pacific crossing in Australia, just 861 miles off the wind.

CHAPTER 6

Australia

We looked back and watched the upscale French city of Nouméa disappear astern—our last island stop on our South Seas crossing from Mexico. We were finally on our way to mainland Australia where LOW KEY could weather cyclone season in relative peace.

There are a couple of considerations when choosing a landing spot in Australia. Most of the cruisers that left New Caledonia and Vanuatu were headed to the port of Bundaberg or Brisbane. I decided to aim further south to arrive at Coff's Harbor. Coff's was closer to our final stop at Sydney but also it was the first check-in port that was not on a river. River port means to me a shallow river-bar entrance that can only be entered twice a day followed by a lot of motoring inland. Also a plus, Coff's reportedly had a more senior and smaller check-in staff (information gleaned from other cruisers via my new long-range radio).

Sailing fast on a southwest course, we quickly found the weather getting cooler. It was time to break out our heavier foulies. We had packed them away six months before, somewhere south of Mexico. Before we left Nouméa we set up a radio net with our friends on MANDARA and SOUTHERN CROSS. On the SSB we checked in daily with the two boats; SOUTHERN CROSS en route to Brisbane and MANDARA still in Nouméa.

With big winds, mostly aft of the beam, the over 800-mile passage went quickly. Only three days out of Nouméa we started to pick up the coastal weather forecasts coming from Australia. It was comforting to have access to hourly updates as we closed with the coast. Indeed, a change of weather was coming. The wind was forecast to back around to the southwest and pick up to thirty knots. This was bad news for us. For the last twenty hours of our ocean crossing we would have to beat straight upwind.

We sailed into it for a while until I noticed the headsail halyard had suffered some chafe, leaving only a few strands holding up the highly loaded sail. I went to plan B. To spare the halyard and to shorten the duration of our upwind suffering, I fired the engine and we did a little motorsailing. With just a reefed down main and the engine we can point much closer to the wind. Our fast progress did not last long.

"Woody, I think the engine is melting," is not what you want to hear when you are just about to go off watch. There was smoke and a smell coming from the engine room. I put it in neutral and poked my head into the ER. I could not see much through the smoke/water vapor, so I just shut it down and went back on deck to pull the headsail up on its nearly parted halyard. We had no spare. I had done a lot for this boat: I felt entitled to a minor miracle now and then.

With all reefs taken in both sails, we plowed into the fury of thirty knots of wind slamming into two knots of opposing current. We clawed our way up the coast and sailed through the pass at Coff's the next morning.

Upon further inspection I found that the aqualift muffler had been installed too close to the hot engine and that the plastic intake had melted and collapsed, sending exhaust into the engine room. It would have been convenient to blame the guy who installed it but unfortunately that guy was me.

In trouble with the man

Dena's "Maybe we should get a tow in . . . ?" comment was received with a blank stare. We received our slip assignment ("berth information" in Oz) from the radio. I sealed up the engine room and fired her up. We pulled into our berth, at the feet of waiting Customs officers, a smoking mess. To further complicate things, in the excitement I had forgotten to put up the yellow Quarantine flag. When arriving in a new country you must put up the yellow Q flag indicating that your crew is healthy and that you are "requesting free pratique." It is an old custom but it is all very much by the letter here in Australia. There was mention of a mandatory fine that, through diligent smiling and "Yes ma'ams," thankfully never materialized. I did watch about 12 kilos of food get carried off in a trash bag. I am a big fan of food, so it was sad to see it go.

Food Czar Dena believed that it would be like all the other countries and we would not be searched. Australia was the first country to search the boat. They went so far as rubbing cotton patches on select surfaces which were then sent in to be measured for traces of illicit substances. The quarantine fee (everyone pays) was $132. On the positive side, they were very nice, and instead of dealing with three groups of people—Quarantine, Immigration, and Customs—it was all done by just the two officers.

It was good to be in a country that we would not be leaving in a week. If all went to plan, LOW KEY would be spending nine months sailing around Australia. I was also relieved to have survived another skirting of hurricane season (it's called cyclone season in the southern hemisphere). I am always telling people that most of those disaster-at-sea stories you hear are about boats that purposely venture out in the wrong season. Checked in, tied to the dock and feeling at ease, we ventured into town to find an ATM and a true Australian pub.

Like I said, it is all by the book around here. The next morning, after a great shower, I ambled up to the Customs office and filled out our cruising permit covering all of our intended stops while visiting Oz. Right downstairs was a proper chandlery where I picked up a new halyard and aqualift, both reasonably priced. I installed the aqualift further away from the engine, aft of the main fuel tank, in previously wasted space.

Moving the aqualift freed up some room around the raw water hoses so I rerouted them, ending up with a cleaner run with easier access. I love it when everything works out perfectly.

I did not have large-scale charts (large on detail) or a good cruising guide for the trip south to Sydney, so I was counting on my computer charts to get us into the bar entrances along the way. While tidying up the boat after arrival in Coff's, I dunked the inverter and thus the ability to charge the laptop. I had about an hour left on the battery. I decided to use most of that time to pull up each of the entrances we would encounter and sketch them onto paper. Sure, it would have been easier to buy more charts, but where's the fun in that? Besides, charts for the run would have set me back about $150 US, more importantly, about 160 Australian beers. Sound fiscal policy.

We were sailing fast, down current, through the night. We wanted to make as much distance as possible before the wind came around onto the nose again. Playing with the SSB on the AM band, I found the Australia vs New Zealand rugby game. Like cross town rivals, the two teams battled it out for the chance to go to the final in the upcoming Rugby World Cup.

With south winds approaching, we pulled into Port Stevens. A lot of the entrances here are framed by large rock formations that protect the inner bays. Port Stevens is considered an all-weather entrance. Other river bar entrances along the coast get shut down during rough weather. At which point the channels become really good places to go surfing.

We parked the boat in a marina and walked up to the office. The guy said that it was free for the afternoon for visiting yachts. Great. He then said it was $56 for the night. Not a chance. If I were to move the boat about 200 feet, than it would be free again. We moved over to the public wharf. We gave up our access to water and . . . that was about it.

It was here that we learned about the RSL clubs. They are veterans' clubs, found in every town, that also admit guests who are visiting from at least 50 kilometers away. We qualified and partook of the cheap coldies and big screen TV showing the "Pommies vs Frogs," as it was billed. The England vs France game was the other semifinal of the rugby. The next night we went over to the Hog's Breath for a "piss up." Dena and I met a couple of Austrian girls and partied into the night.

After re-wiring the laptop to run on 12 volts and loading up on some VB (Victoria Bitter, the popular beer in these parts), we sailed out into another fair wind. We sailed south, with dolphins coming and going at the bow, until the next morning. We were just north of the entrance to Sydney (Port Jackson), where boat traffic was thick, when we hit fog—for the first time on the voyage. I headed the boat in toward shore using the depth sounder and the chart as a guide. I knew that there would be more fishing boats near shore, but I was more worried about the big tankers we had been watching plow up and down the coast. The water was too shallow for them inshore.

My only other defense was our CARD unit (Collision Avoidance Radar Detector). LOW KEY does not have radar. This is the only time on the circumnavigation I would have used it. We had used the CARD casually many times before, but now we really needed it. It worked. It spotted a tanker just off the port bow. A few minutes later, I heard it go by. It did not give us a whole lot of warning, but it would have been plenty of time to get the offending vessel on the radio to make sure they knew where we were.

Just as we made the turn into where I imagined the entrance to Sydney to be, the fog began to clear away. Close up, I could see both North Head and South Head which proudly guard the opening to renowned Sydney Harbour, the place where LOW KEY would enjoy a three-month break from ocean voyaging. Being used to sighting landfall from far away, it was very cool indeed to have those great landmarks appear so suddenly and auspiciously.

As we passed into the relative safety of the harbor, I thought about the great distance that LOW KEY had covered in the last seven months. I was very proud of my little blue sloop and, of course, her intrepid crew of two.

CHAPTER 7

Sydney Harbour

The morning fog gave way to a clear blue sky as we worked our way through day sailers, giant ferry traffic and the many navigation buoys. Down a ways and around a corner, we approached downtown Sydney with skyscrapers, more ferries and a big bridge over the funny shell-shaped building. We cruised under the bridge and dropped the hook in a nook called Ball's Head Bay.

Ball's Head was otherwise known as the International Anchorage which is Australian for "tourists must park here." It turned out to be a great spot. The little bay is surrounded by a national park area with an island on the left and a beach on the right. I found our new home to be secure in all winds. Up the hill is Wollstonecraft, an upscale Sydney suburb with its own rail station to the city. Walk further up the road and you'll find a town called Crow's Nest with stores and pubs, and even a chandlery. It is also the home of Boat Books, the largest marine bookshop in Australia. I would get to know Crow's Nest well.

The list of projects that LOW KEY required was long. After securing the boat, Dena and I tossed aside the work list and headed into the city where we found a map, chips (fries), and a few pints of Ozzie brew at a cool place on the wharf of touristy Darling Harbour. Just across the walkway, a live band was setting up on a big charter boat; timing is every-thing.

Since approaching the coast of Australia, I had been tuning into the Rugby World Cup games. A couple of days after our arrival in Sydney, they held the Rugby final. For the first time in forever, the Pommies (English) had a chance to take the cup back to the northern hemisphere. A reported 12,000 fans flew down from England to cheer their team on. Dena and I caught the game in a little suburb called King's Cross.

The Cross is as seedy as Sydney gets, with massage parlors, brothels, and live sex show venues going 24/7. For some reason there are also a lot of backpacker hostel/pubs in the same area. The combination keeps the scene pretty cheery. We found a sports bar with cheap pitchers and settled in. Sports betting is big in Australia. We placed a losing bet on the underdog and leaned back to view the carnage. The Rugby final was a good game but it did not hold a candle to the entertainment value of the clash between the English and Australian fans in the bar. By the end of the night, I couldn't understand in what language either of them were shouting.

Back in our little bay there were a few boats. One stood out. It was a big powerboat of trawler design, U.S.-flagged, from Rhode Island. NEVER NEVER LAND was a long way from home. It was not long before a proper yacht tender pulled alongside LOW KEY with a jolly, tanned older guy driving. I found out that Ron and his lovely wife, Janice, were motoring around the world backwards (eastward) and that they would like to have us over for dinner. How nice is that?

Wow, air conditioning. And I didn't bring a sweatshirt. You forget all about excesses like AC when you cruise at our pace. NEVER NEVER LAND had three large staterooms with TVs and VCRs, four heads, a full shop, a walk-in engine room, a galley that you would find in a townhouse, a cool pilothouse, a fly-bridge, and a patio on the back. Those were all nice but the best part, as far as I was concerned, was the saloon setup. Across from the big TV was a real couch with a bonus: Both ends of the couch had recliners. "And how many movies?" I had to ask. Four hundred was the answer.

And then there was one

And after almost eight months of living and sailing together on LOW KEY, Dena and I decided that she would head home, indefinitely. We had been planning it for months and when other cruisers would hear about it they would tell us how every cruising couple had problems blah blah blah. They didn't understand. We weren't married; we hadn't made an eternal promise to stay together. Neither of us were prepared for the consequences of having two very passionate people living together in the close quarters that cruising demands. Most of the time it was truly great. But when it turned bad, our differences seemed irreconcilable. She flew back to Los Angeles, collected her dog, bought a van and started some stateside land-cruising.

Back on NEVER NEVER LAND, Ron was also left by himself. Janice had flown home to visit family as she did a couple times a year. Ron is a social guy and he likes to tell his stories. I found out he had a lot of them. I spent many an evening on NEVER NEVER LAND having a beer or three, watching a movie, and then listening to Ron's stories on everything from running a successful company to cold war submarines. It was like school, only on NEVER NEVER LAND the subject matter was more interesting.

Normally, it would drive me crazy to be in one place for more than a day or two—a habit I'd picked up from Bob Bitchin. Basically, I was trapped in the south by cyclone season. I figured I could survive with Sydney close by to entertain me, and of course there was plenty to do on the boat. LOW KEY needed a mini refit. It is a strange fact of maintaining a boat that as soon as you set out to fix one thing, a series of other projects become apparent. As you tackle the job list, for a while, the list only gets longer. Lucky for LOW KEY, I would have the time now to tend to her.

A sampling of boat projects for the curious

I took the wind generator down and smoothed and polished the blades. I painted a mini U.S. flag on each side of the tail so I could take down the fabric flag. After a thorough inspection of the engine I tightened the dipstick fitting, changed a loose hose clamp on the new aqualift, and tightened an engine mount bolt. I installed the new tiller extension (we had worn the old one out). I built a portable backup bilge pump. To use it, I drop the pump into the bilge, toss the end of the hose into the cockpit, and plug the cord into the 12-volt outlet. I reinstalled the rubrails (PVC tubing cut in half) that had been torn off by the sea. To prevent it from happening again, I used throughbolts in the bow, filled the forward ends with Multicaulk, and fitted end caps. A dry boat is an important thing. They say it's impossible, that all cruising boats leak. Forget that theory. By Sydney, LOW KEY only had a couple of small drips but I took the time to fix them. I inspected the rig and moved the radar reflector away from the mast. The monster spinnaker pole needed a new end. In order to free the old end from the pole, I tied both the end fitting and the pole, each to a winch, and cranked the winches as tight as I could. I then heated the joint with the torch and hit the area with a hammer. The end had no choice but to come off. Since losing the inverter in a careless accident, I have been attempting to wean the boat off inverter-made 110 volts. The last step was acquiring a 12-volt charger for the digital camera batteries and now the transformation was complete.

City life

Spare time is like a vacuum; soon I had plenty to do. When not busy with the boat, I would walk up to Crow's Nest for supplies, do e-mail, and check out the pubs where I would pretend to enjoy cricket. Each time I went to the city I would try to explore a different section. I would usually end up at the big market. I would go there to get vegetables, but they also had a whole flea market going on. For the first time in a year I had my hair cut. Long hair can get in the way when it's squally out. Oil filters for LOW KEY's Volvo diesel were $25 at home. I found automotive oil filters that fit the threads and the seal from an Oz K-mart for $5.50. It is not something I recommend to you, but I thought I'd try it. I've since experienced no ill effects. FYI: My replacement alternator (built for a GM truck) that I got for $29 is still going strong.

After finishing up downtown one day, I found the trains had stopped running. There was some kind of gas leak in the tunnels. It was a beautiful day and all of central Sydney was in a semi-panic. The streets were packed with people walking, trying to get to somewhere they could catch public transportation out. I decided that a pub crawl was in order. I started with the pub in front of me. Every couple of blocks I would pull into another pub, bring together a window seat and a coldy, and sit back to watch the frantic business district scurry by. I finally got to walk across the Harbour Bridge, though the memory is a little fuzzy.

Back on the boat, I cracked open the mini recipe book that Dena had prepared for me and I learned how to make pizza. Is there anything else one needs to know about cooking? Ron and I had pizza for Christmas.

On Boxing Day, the day after Christmas, Ron picked me up in the NNL tender and we jetted out to watch the start of the famous Sydney to Hobart race. It was very cool. After the big boats headed out to sea, we toured a couple of the bays inland. On the way back we rescued a couple of girls who were stranded on an anchored boat and took them back to their yacht club. Maybe I needed a big yacht tender.

Sydney was having the world's largest fireworks show for New Year's Eve. I sailed up the harbor the day before and tried to find a good spot to view the show. The anchorage cordoned off by the Waterways people for us spectator boats did not allow shore access. How would I resupply provisions or tempt lovely passers-by? Captain Ron had invited me to their yacht for New Year's Eve. He was having his Australian friends (hereafter referred to as "the guys") over for a BBQ and to watch the fireworks from the upper deck. I invited this hot Norwegian babe I met on my beach and, of course, she brought her boyfriend. The guys were flight attendants for Quantas. Throughout the evening Ron and I listened to the stories they had accumulated from flying for the last few decades. During the course of the evening I deduced that being a straight male flight attendant must be one of the greatest occupations ever.

The guys adopted me, showed me Sydney, and invited me into their homes to enjoy their parties, BBQs, swimming pools, TV, Internet and daughters. They took me to their favorite outdoor eatery where feral women (their words) abound. I ordered the kangaroo and, reluctantly, so did one of the guys. Apparently there is a cartoon roo that they all grew up with named Skippy. Our friend got sick, from the guilt of eating Skippy we assumed.

On weekends I would sail around and find a new beach to anchor off. There are many amazing spots in Sydney Harbour. I took one of the guys for a sail and anchored off one of the perfect beaches. I rowed the stern hook in to shore so I could back the boat up to the beach, offering us a better view. We were in the perfect spot, sipping on some coldies and thinking about heading in to get some lunch when a small powerboat pulled up next to us. The one guy and his four young female crew were getting ready to anchor. Being the gentleman sailor that I am, I offered to let them side tie, which they did for the afternoon.

Another boat pulled into my bay. It was a 38-foot Catalina from California called PANDEMONIUM. Dave had crossed the Pacific on basically the same route as LOW KEY. We knew all of the same cruisers. It was amazing that we had never crossed paths. Dave's business partner lived in raging Bondi Beach on the eastside of Sydney. Dave was staying at her house for the season, only coming out to the bay to work on the boat. On more than one occasion I was tempted to knock off work early and join Dave in a bottle of some kind of booze he had collected on his journeys. Dave turned out to be a good guy to know. His partner had friends. Dave started bringing down hot babes that wanted to go bay sailing. He always needed help. They would go by the fish market and the girls would pick up fresh prawns and some sides, ever thankful for the chance to get out on the bay. We would tack up and park off one of the many great beaches for lunch and a swim. As the sun set, we would sail back down the harbor, drifting under the bridge at night. It was fun to see them appreciate something that I often took for granted.

Dave had an old car and we drove out to the used boat parts place one day. As I was paying for my new used tiller pilot, a local walked up and asked if I was Captain Woody. Turns out he was one of my seven fans. You would have to be a true fan of *Latitudes & Attitudes* if you were paying Australian $13 (U.S. $10) an issue. I told Mick about the *Latitudes & Attitudes* party we were throwing in the Whitsundays, June 12. He knew about it and was fired up.

Like home

Then I found Manly Beach. Manly is a town at the north end of long Sydney Harbour, north of the entrance heads. It has a nice little cove beach to anchor off on the inside of the bay. Ashore there is a street closed to traffic where it is all happening. There are shops and bars and hostels and all of the ingredients for a great little beach town. It reminded me of my town, Hermosa Beach, back home. At the other end of town is the ocean beach with surf and volleyball and topless sunbathers.

I first sailed up to Manly to check out a pro beach volleyball tournament held on the ocean beach. A guy named Dane got second place in the tournament. Dane used to play VB with my friend Eric. The two of them got the gold in the Sydney Olympics in 2000.

On my dinghy row back to LOW KEY, I stopped to talk to a

guy on a big catamaran. It was here that I met my new idol. The sailing cat SHAGUAR was owned by Ken. Ken was a self-made brewmaster. Ken had his brewery onboard, complete with a refer that held three mini kegs. We partook of numerous home-brewed coldies from a real tap as Ken told me his story. This started me thinking. . . .

Sometime after Tahiti, we broke a wire in the port upper shroud, one of the cables that holds up the mast. Somewhere in Sydney Harbour I broke another. I decided not to wait until the rig came down to replace the shrouds. Finding a master rigger in Sydney was not difficult. The old guy explained to me that the first broken wire is a warning. The second broken wire requires some of the load to be removed through deep reefing. A third break and you need to take all weight off the rig by tacking over so you can limp in to your rigger. He asked where I was headed. I told him I was going to cross the Indian Ocean next. Ignoring my complaints of weight aloft, he made up my new rigging two sizes larger.

To get up the mast, I use the preventer block and tackle, extended with a super long line. I attach one block to the bosun's chair and pull the other to the top of the mast with the main halyard. With a four to one purchase, I can hoist myself up the mast and tie off. So there I am, at the top of the mast replacing my shrouds, when the wind picks up. A sick feeling ran through me when I heard a flutter, then a thump, and the wind generator suddenly went silent. I looked down to see my climbing line wrapped up in the wind mill. The wind was strong enough to blow the line back over the stern and into the spinning blades. I finished up the rigging job before trying to figure out how I would get down without any line to feed into the block and tackle. It was another beautiful day and I could see for miles up the bay. But lunch time would be upon me soon, so a slight panic began to settle in. Climbing out of the chair at the top of the mast and trying to climb down did not seem to be an option. I flagged down a sportfisher. The guys looked up, pointed, and just laughed as they putted by. That exchange brought out a guy from a ketch nearby who rowed over and methodically unraveled my mess. I got back to the deck just as the guy was trying to escape. I thanked him. I later learned that the other cruisers called the mysterious man who rarely emerged from his vessel, "The Count." His ketch was the MONTE CRISTO.

It would seem that exploring the U.S. by camper van was not as exciting as cruising the world. After three months, Dena and I were talking about her coming back. She wanted to go back to school but would put it off to do some more cruising. Looking back, our disputes seemed minor and Dena was always great crew. After leaving Sydney, the boat would be moving pretty fast and her company would be especially valuable. We worked some things out over the phone, and she flew in two weeks later for another go.

The seasons were beginning to turn in southern Australia. It was starting to get cooler, and the storms barreling down from the north were becoming less frequent. As great as Sydney was, it was time to go. After a couple of days getting reacquainted, Dena and I sailed over to Manly Beach to get closer to the Sydney Harbour entrance. We cleaned the bottom of the boat so we would be fast. The rig was stronger, the small leaks were fixed, and a new storm headsail was at the ready. We were looking forward to putting to sea again, even if just for the four-day sail north to the Gold Coast and Surfers Paradise.

CHAPTER 8

Underway Down Under

After four months in one bay waiting out the cyclone season, we were ready to get moving again. We spent our last days in Sydney visiting and saying goodbye to our many new friends. We met them at pubs and attended send off BBQs and received wishes for good winds and safe passages.

It was the dead of night (as always) when I heard the loud crunching noise and felt the boat shudder. We were anchored in the cove at Manly, perched near the entrance to Sydney Harbour, awaiting the southern winds that would whisk us north. The south wind had arrived and it was now conspiring with the stern anchor to pull us into a shark net enclosure (for swimmers). From a deep sleep, I emerged on deck to see our heavy windvane steering gear chipping away at the cement corner post. The post was loosing the battle. I eased the stern rode and we drifted away from impending doom.

Now was as good a time as any to get started. I collected our anchors, secured the dinghy on the foredeck and hoisted the sails. Dena and I sailed out through the towering black headlands, finally leaving Sydney astern. We had a nice quiet sail that night, beam reaching in 15 knots of wind. Nessie, unfazed by her encounter with the post, was steering stellarly. The winds were forecast to lighten up for a couple of days so we altered course and made our way back toward shore to pull into Port Stephens. We arrived at night and sailed in with the tide, a light wind pushing from astern. The only sound was from the occasional venting dolphin close abeam.

We parked at the public wharf again. We were not in Port Stephens long. It is not a very exciting town. We filled with water, did e-mail, bought food and caught a movie. Dena made pizza for the crew of MISTY BLUE. Baz was the father of James and Ash who had been raised on the boat. When not in school, the family cruised the east coast of Australia. What a cool way to grow up. And then, before I could get my snooker lesson from Baz, the wind piped up from the south again and we were off.

This part of the Australian coast has a two-knot current running from north to south. We had a strong wind blowing from south to north. When wind fights current, seas get unruly. It was strange sailing. The not so big waves were breaking over each other, making for a bumpy ride, but also allowing us to surf from time to time. With the help of the breaking seas, a light boat like LOW KEY can get pushed past its hull speed. This forces her up onto a plane and causes her to slide off down the wave at much higher speeds. This should have made us go fast, but with a knot or two of current against us, our average speed stayed low. It was a long couple of days, doing less than 100 miles a day. I was starting to think that maybe sailing downwind was not all that great (did I say that?). And then we rounded Cape Byron and everything changed. As soon as we left the counter current behind us, the sea mellowed, and LOW KEY shot off at her normal cruising speed—a humble 5 to 6 knots.

We arrived at Southport in the wee hours. Dena had just come off watch so I didn't wake her. I brought the sails down and fired up our old Volvo diesel. A local cruiser had advised us to pass by the main anchorage in Bumís Bay and park closer to town. It was dark, but as I made my way past Bumís, I could see that it was full of cruisers (read: soon-to-be friends). I decided to park there for the night. We anchored across from our old friends on NEVER NEVER LAND. Ron and Janice were glad to see us. Ron, having an inexhaustible desire to cruise the waterways in his yacht tender, offered to show us around. Perfect! We cruised most of the southern reaches, including a stop in Surfers

Paradise for a jug of coldies at an Irish pub overlooking the tanned bodies on the main beach.

While in Bumís Bay we met Rick and Mary on TRANQUILITY. Mary was a computer guru and had run various weather nets on the SSB radio. I had tuned into one of her nets after leaving Fiji. TRANQUILITY has helped hundreds of cruisers. The two helped me to fine tune my software. We also exchanged movies. To Dena's delight, the VHS tapes that Rick was pawning were the entire first season of *Sex and the City*. It took two nights and many buckets of popcorn (and quite a few coldies) to make it through the set. Note: When leaving the U.S., it is good to have a multi-system DVD player (NTSC and PAL with all regions 1-6).

We sailed up the coast to Mooloolaba and got the hook down just before sunset. The place was crawling with mini-mansions. I gave up pizza night onboard for the $7 All-You-Can-Eat at the bowling club uptown. Being visitors from more than 50 kilometers away, the club had to let us in. What a great system! Dena and I got there early and had a jug (a pitcher) at the bar as I distractedly eyed my food being prepared at the other end of the club.

Like a sea of southern plantation owners, the white-clad lawn bowlers came in from the fields. One of them took an interest in us and asked all about our voyage. I warned him about the pending carnage about to occur in the dining room between the buffet and me. Roger was the president of the club and he welcomed us to it.

Since it had been a somewhat uneventful month, we decided to try something that always gets us into trouble—an inside passage. Ever since I took a boat up that ridiculous Intracoastal Waterway on the east coast of the U.S., I have successfully avoided long days of motoring through shallow murky waters, being led by the nose from buoy to buoy. It requires too much concentration for too long a time and rates low on the Captain Woody fun meter. But being older (almost 35 now) and hopefully wiser (nowhere to go but up), I was ready to try it again.

To get into the 40nm cut between Frasier Island and the marshy mainland, you must first traverse the gauntlet—an ugly patch of water zigzagging between breaking shoals led by a directional beacon followed by a range (leading lights). It was advanced navigation to be sure. True to form, LOW KEY arrived seaward of the treacherous pass at night. I don't mind night arrivals. Sometimes it is easier to make out markers when they are lit up and flashing. In this case though, I would have liked to be able to see the breaking waves that I could hear thundering nearby.

We sailed across the face of the island until we found the red sector of the beacon. This meant that we were still to port of the safe channel—red left returning in Oz. When we crossed into the white (safe water) sector, we turned LOW KEY in toward land. Soon, the moon dropped behind the island and the only thing I could see was the beacon, a couple lights from homes ashore and some city lights far off down the coast. And suddenly there were waves breaking just to starboard. Waves mean shallow water. I maneuvered to port slightly. It seemed the beacon needed some adjustment. Then the waves started breaking off to port. We could hear them but could only see the white of the breaking parts. The channel was tight. I couldn't have turned around if I wanted to. Dena, having just finished making pizza, came up into the cockpit to witness the chaos. True to form, she seemed unfazed, excited even, probably assuming I knew what I was doing. Looking back, I was in the same mindset as Dena, trusting the navigationally precise Aussies had their lights in order. We motored straight along our thin stretch of calmer water.

Soon the second light range came into view way off to port. The two lights began to align which indicated it was time for us to start our turn. The only problem was that the waves were still breaking just to port. I hesitated. But knowing that if I held our current course we would end up on the beach, I took a leap of faith and turned us hard to port. What was the worst that could happen? Dena was an excellent swimmer. Through the dark night we watched the first crashing breaker approach LOW KEY. Just before rolling over us, the wave flattened out and pushed under the boat. We were in the deep water. Looking ahead along our shoreline route, we could see the peaks of large breaking waves as they blocked out far-off city lights. I hoped that the swells would not still be breaking where they crossed our path.

And suddenly it was calm. We had made it to the tranquil water inside the shoals. In the pitch black night we tried to find a place to anchor. I was just about to park right there on the side of the channel when I spotted the low stars off to port. They were not stars but anchor lights at the tops of the masts of other sailboats. With the depth sounder as our navigator, we slowly felt our way over to them and dropped the hook.

At first light, and on a rising tide, we headed off on our inland adventure. Lack of vigilance is the enemy on a buoy-to-buoy inland cruise. The channel started out a kilometer wide. I was having trouble finding the first channel marker. And then I spotted it . . . way off to port. In a don't worry kind of tone, I said, "Isn't that . . . ?" and we oozed to a stop. We had run into a big muddy shoal.

The water rushing into the channel had LOW KEY pinned to the shoal. I could not coax the bow around to motor off. We launched the dinghy and I rowed out and dropped a kedge (the stern anchor with its nylon rode run through the bow). I led the rode back to a cockpit winch via an opening sheet block and cranked us around into the current. A couple more cranks and we eased out of the muck. No longer leaving it up to me, Dena started to pay more attention to the particulars of our course after that.

After a very long, though scenic, day we finally parked in the lee of an island that sat out in the middle of a wide part of the passage. We were tired, but that did not stop Dena from wanting to see Big Woody, which was the name of the island. To catch the tide out, we left our private island paradise at midnight and sailed into the deeper Hervey Bay.

LOW KEY was expecting a guest in a few days. Aaron was a reader of *Latitudes & Attitudes* and was going to meet up with us at a town called Bundaberg. Bundaberg lies 10 miles up a river. Twice in one week I would be called upon to overextend my navigational skills. We arrived at the base of the Burnett River while the tide-driven current was still flowing out. We pulled off the river into a tiny marina to kill some time. I parked at the end of a dock and asked the nice man where we could garner a coldy to pass the time until the tide turned around. He pointed across the water to a yellow building he said was the Burnett Heads Rowing Club.

Well, the rowers had long ago abandoned that hole in the wall. Still, we liked the place so we had a couple of jugs while sitting across from some entertaining one-kangaroo-town locals. They were great to us. They put money in the jukebox insisting that Dena pick the songs. Before we left, they gave us pub tips for when we arrived up stream: "Don't go to Gary's 'less you want to get in a fight," said one. "Go to Central if you want DJ music and $6.50 jugs," said another. I asked if there was a cover charge. I got blank stares.

We motored off the dock and headed up the Burnett River. I would call it more of a creek than a river. The flood tide did not start running until 5:00 pm. So once again, there we were, tooling around in the dark. The buoys were easy to spot. They were all lit up and blinking, and this time, they were closer together. The night was perfect. It was warm, still and clear. The Southern Cross was high in the sky. The faint glow of Bundaberg was far off over the low marsh landscape. Being swept up the creek in the fast moving current, we just sat back and enjoyed the ride. Besides the occasional campfire ashore, there was no one else around. For some reason, no one else was trying to run the creek at night.

I saw it coming—there was a disturbance in the water up ahead. I was in the lane, right where I was supposed to be, so I didn't slow down. We hit it. It was some kind of narrow sand bank speed bump. The boat barely slowed as it pushed through and motored on. As we passed the big Bundaberg Distillery, we could smell the sweet fragrance of fermenting rum. Two more bends and we drifted into downtown Bundaberg. It was smaller than I had expected and quiet, but I liked it right away. It had a good feel. We anchored in the middle of flowing waterway.

CHAPTER 9

En route to the Whitsundays

We had a guest coming. Dena and I were in middle Queensland where big coastal ports were few and far between. We had brought LOW KEY ten miles up a river to the town of Bundaberg so we could clean up and stock the boat, knock out a couple boat projects, and do the rum distillery tour. Bundaberg was also the only place in the area with a rail station which made it possible for our guest to meet up with us.

There is one marina in the town of Bundaberg. It has docks and weird end-to-end moorings to keep boats aligned with the tidal flow of the river. The cruising guide mentioned that cruisers could anchor down river, outside of town. We had arrived at night and had parked LOW KEY in what seemed like a perfect spot, in the middle of town.

Why is it that cruisers are more likely to be found walking around naked? Is it the sense of freedom that cruising instills? Is it a habit brought in from the seclusion of the sea? At first light, I came out on deck to find a guy on a boat across the way, standing in his cockpit naked and staring at LOW KEY. He disappeared below when he saw me. Later, when Adrian and Gerta were having coffee in their cockpit (clothed), I rowed over. The Dutch couple were concerned that the big marina would not approve of my parking spot. I explained how we were just in town to provision and pick up a guest. They suggested that we park on the nice private dock they were on. It would have been rude to say no.

Adrian and Gerta cruise the GBR (Great Barrier Reef) during the good winter season and live at the dock during the summer cyclone season. The owners of the dock were John, Sharon and Monty. John was a local prawn fisherman (no such thing as 'shrimp on the barbie' in Oz). Sharon, his wife, came from the States. Monty is a beefy little sheep terrier that patrols the dock and provides comedy.

Our five new friends made us feel right at home. Gerta took Dena and introduced her to a real washing machine in a shack onshore. The next day the two drove into town to provision. Adrian and I just sat around and drank beers on the dock all day . . . oh, and cleaned up and fixed some things on LOW KEY. Adrian was a welder and took it upon himself to fix my spinnaker pole end which had seized up. He then had a look at our dock cart and decided that it could use a rebuild. We went and picked up some stainless rod and pipe. Then Adrian, John and I, laden with a few coldies, headed off to the welding shed to "work." While staying at the dock, Dena and I got a tour of a working prawn boat, a visit to the bat estuary, attended a fish fry, and copied a set of charts that would take us all the way to Darwin.

The day came that our guest Aaron was to arrive. We were cleaned up and provisioned and awaiting his arrival on a mooring at the big marina (as per the plan). The boys must have missed us already because they pulled up alongside. John and Adrian were in the coolest little river boat powered by an exposed, one-cylinder Spanish diesel inboard. I asked them to come aboard of course. Patiently waiting for Aaron, we went through most of his arrival coldies which inspired the boys to go back to the dock for Gerta and a bottle of Bundy Rum. Aaron was a no show. So after the rum was gone, we all went out to the local pub for two-for-one dinners.

The next day I got the news that Aaron was having trouble getting a flight out of the States. He was a pilot and was flying standby. After another day that Aaron could not get out, he decided to put off his sailing vacation. So what do you do when you have a boat full of food and beer and a pocket full of loose change (Aaron's deposit)? You head out to the islands—after a farewell dock party. If you are ever in Bundaberg and want to meet some great people and park in a great spot (half the price of a mid-town mooring), head over to the blue floating dock next to the boat yard and tell them Woody sent you.

With half a moon to light our way, we motored down the creek of bugs and out into the ocean. It was nice to feel the sea breeze and the mellow swell heaving under us again. We were not in a hurry. We had 50 miles to go and 12 hours to arrive at the atoll Lady Musgrave. I had the whomper up (our 155% deck-sweeping headsail) and poled out on our "new" pole to port. Dena woke me at 0300, the only time anything interesting seems to happen. It's funny how things always seem so calm from down below. I arrived on deck to find we had sailed into a ton of wind. I struggled with it but eventually got the whomper down. I looked around. With no sail up, we were doing four knots with Nessie tracking along like a champ. Purrfect, we would arrive about 0900 with enough light to navigate the reefs at Lady Musgrave.

A quick note: I am sure everyone already knows about the value of polarized lenses in a reef setting. I had always heard about them but never owned any until my friend Keith gave me a pair in Fiji. Now I always switch to my X-ray vision glasses when venturing into reefy areas.

There was a really strong current running out of the narrow pass to Lady Musgrave. We had to run LOW KEY up the slower water along the side of the pass just to make headway. It is in times like these that you take comfort in your frequent attention to the engine. If it had died right then, well—it would have been a bumpy ride back out the pass.

It is one of my favorite things—coming in from a feisty sea and dropping the hook down through calm clear water, watching it fall on powder white sand and settling back securely at anchor. It had been a long time since we had seen coral sand and perfect water with a soon-to-be-explored palm island close abeam.

The reef island had been tended by the Australian forest service. We followed a white sand foot path on its winding route through the center of the island. The lush trees provided a canopy which kept things cool while the swooping, playful bird life kept us entertained. On the other side was a small campsite complete with a big hand pump that sucked freshwater from the island's core.

With the shore excursion out of the way, we went swimming. Well, Dena snorkeled over to the reef and I cleaned the river dirt off the bottom of the boat. I took the next day and installed the lights in the boat. I know it sounds crazy, but with a plug-in 12-volt shoplight and a really cool lantern, we hadn't missed having installed lights all that much. Working on the boat was fun there. It was an ideal setting. The boat was flat with the breeze flowing through keeping things cool. Mix in a little music and you've got perfect working conditions.

We finally tore ourselves away from paradise—so much still to see. On LOW KEY, a departure day goes something like this: I get up and check the weather on the SSB. While Dena is whipping up some breakfast, I consult the paper or computer charts and extract the lats and longs of waypoints that will lead us safely to our destination. I enter the waypoints into the GPS. I also enter the location of dangers on each side of our track so we know what side to favor and when. I figure a destination ETA from the GPS info and, if necessary, adjust our departure time to compensate for tidal issues. This Australia place has a lot of river bars that you must hit on the flood (arriving during the day is a bonus but no longer factors into our departure timing). While Dena secures cabin-based projectiles and clinking things, I go on deck to make sure everything is right and to set up one of the sails.

In the Musgrave case, the pass was downwind. I set up a headsail, ready to be hoisted in case the engine failed in the rapids. I checked the oil, fired the engine, turned up the refer and flipped on the instruments. I pulled the hook and secured the dinghy as we headed over to the pass. It was a quick exit with the current pushing us to nine knots. Once out, I pulled up the headsail and set up Nessie. Sailing down our course at six plus knots there was nothing to do but grab a book.

We stopped at Great Keppel and checked out the resorts. A dilemma had arisen that I did not find an immediate solution for. We had 10 days and all of the Whitsunday Islands to see. We had enough food and water for weeks. The problem was that we only had about 12 beers left. We could probably survive, but what if we had friends over? I would do it for them, the poor sods. We headed over to Rosslyn Bay on the mainland to pick up another case or two. We discovered that nowhere in Rosslyn could you buy beer (even at the freak beerless marina). Fortunately, it was Mother's Day and a nice conversation with Mom was enough to comfort me in my time of distress.

We hit a couple more islands before finding Pearl Bay. It was a rocky, breezy approach with a lot of turns but we made it in and anchored up. What a nice spot. It was well protected with thick trees behind a nice, long running beach. We met some cruisers here who had a spunky miniature dog called Jack Daniels. They let us take him ashore and he wore us out. Like playing with your friends' kids, he was hilarious, for a couple of hours.

To make it to our next island destination at the right time, we had to leave Pearl in the darkest part of the night. To shorten our trip, I wanted to head out the shoal-strewn north entrance. To save us some guesswork, I took the dinghy around during the day with a handline and plotted an exit track on the GPS. It must have worked because we didn't hit anything on the way out.

On a deserted beach at Middle Percy Island, they have an A-frame building where cruisers can leave their mark. Most paint signs on driftwood or leave a piece of their boat with details inscribed thereon. There were hundreds of these cruising brands in both the A-frame and the little building next to it. There was also a two-story tree house on the hill that begged exploration. I installed our *Latitudes and Attitudes* burgee in the A-frame, we checked the tree house before heading back out to sea.

A couple islands later we pulled into Refuge Bay at Scawfell Island. As we entered the bay, Dena made me slow down so we would not run over one of the many big sea turtles. Though our chef was a vegetarian, I found it hard to suppress thoughts of turtle soup, filet of turtle, tacos de turtle, turtleini. . . .

Scawfell was a serious island. From the long beach ashore, the hills shot way up into the sky, lush and green. It was 10:00 am but we decided to celebrate our entrance into the Whitsundays with a couple of coldies and some Eric Stone tunes—another perfect afternoon. We met Rob on a Cal 40 from San Francisco and with both boats low on coldies, I decided to break out a smuggled bottle of white tequila. It was well received.

The next day was the mandatory hangover-helping reef snorkel, where I nearly ran into a brown, thorny, flat, shark-lookin' thing. It looked like I felt. That night, Dena and I had sundowners on a big, beautiful Amel ketch with Sydneysiders Ron and Heather—the good life.

CHAPTER 10

Desperate Times

The Whitsundays are the islands that most people picture when they think of the Great Barrier Reef. We had finally arrived. We had begun our Whitsunday Islands cruise short on brew, and I don't mean coffee. The cruising guide mentioned an upscale resort island up ahead called Hamilton that could be called upon for "emergency stores." I was thinking this qualified. We bumped into a charter boat (not literally) that was coming out of the marina and got answers to our questions: Where was the "bottle shop" and how close to it could we park the dinghy? I didn't bother to ask how much it was to stay in the marina. We anchored across the channel and dinghied in.

Hamilton was nice. Although it was a private island, they created a cool little town with shops that had high wooden fronts with big lettering, old school western style. Up from the beautiful Sunsail Charter area was the nicest shower facility we had seen in a while. Showering on deck is fine, even fun, but harder to get away with in more crowded areas. It just so happened that Dena and I had brought in our shower stuff and a change of clothes—you never know.

Clean, mean and keen for a coldy, we stopped by the best marina view cafe and absorbed the ambiance while doing our best "just a couple of high-end tourists on vacation" impersonations. We were planning on stopping just for the beer and then jamming over to the cruisers' anchorage on the next island, but we decided instead to hang out for the day. What do you do with some spare time and a whole island to explore? Rent a golf buggy, of course. We had a great time.

After Hamilton, we sailed over to the cruisers' bay called Cid Harbour on Whitsunday Island. It was a great, well protected, tree-lined anchorage with no facilities; a perfect contrast to our Hamilton foray. That evening, we set up the folding canvas chairs on the foredeck, and Natalie Cole helped us to endure another perfect sundowner.

While parked at Cid, we met a couple who were on the last day of their sailboat charter. He was a chef and they owned an inn. Their dream was to one day sail off on their own boat. Before heading back to their shoreside existence, they dropped their extra food into our dinghy. Unlike my chef, this guy was not a vegetarian, and so I was treated to some kind of veal product, the quality of which I have not the palate to fully appreciate, though appreciate it for its meat content, I did. Dena found sun dried tomatoes and a bunch of other peculiar, though premium, pantry products which seemed to make her very excited.

Home away from home

After a ripping sail through small islands, we found ourselves on the approach to the mainland's Airlie Beach and racing a schooner full of backpackers. We were winning . . . for a while. We sailed up and dropped the hook in front of the Whitsunday Sailing Club, among a sea of moored boats. We took the dinghy in and parked at the Club. On the balcony was a guy wearing a *Latitudes & Attitudes* hat. I walked out and gave him the "nice hat" observation. It was Phil, known as Subz on the *Latitudes & Attitudes* bulletin board. Phil had helped me out when I was in Sydney by finding and sending me some haul-out quotations I needed for a visa extension. Phil was excited to see us, and after philling us with yacht club brand coldies, he and his beautiful wife Sue dragged us back to their not so humble abode for tea with the family. Tea? I never saw any tea. Just a lot of great food which closely resembled dinner. On their very cool veranda overlooking their jungly backyard, we had more coldies amongst tikis, torchlight, and Buffett music. Dena and I were persuaded to stay the night.

Phil had also volunteered to be my shipping address in Oz. He had collected six new issues of *Latitudes & Attitudes* that the main office sent out to me. Had it been that long since my last fix? Also, I had found a Sunglass Hut in Sydney and had given them my precious, though broken, pair of Ray-Ban's and told them my situation. Expecting nothing, I arrived at Phil's place to find a new pair waiting for me. A big thank you to Sunglass Hut and Ray-Ban!

A guest

We had a paying guest coming. Guests are good to have. They give a fresh perspective on how great your cruising life is and, of course, the extra money goes a long way out here. A couple of days before, in the heat of a "discussion" (about money of all things), Dena threatened to leave again in Airlie. I held her to it. The break would do us good. She went interviewing other cruising boats the next day. She quickly found a boat that would take her around to islands I intended to skip. LOW KEY and I would have to skip some cool stuff to make up time lost chartering and being hauled in the boatyard.

In the mean time, Phil had arranged for a slip for LOW KEY in the nice marina. Guest preparations (including food provisioning, boat washdown, water filling, etc.) were all made easy by being dockside.

I would be picking up the guest back at Hamilton Island. I took Phil's 15-year-old son Mike, and his Grandad John, along for the ride to Hamilton. Unfortunately, the sail would be to windward. When not on a schedule you have the luxury of waiting out a wind direction change or even changing your destination to avoid sailing upwind. Needing to get to Hamilton that day, Mike and John got to see LOW KEY in a rare beating situation. Sailing in the shelter of the many islands kept the windchop down. They seemed to enjoy the afternoon of sailing. I dropped Mike and John at the dock in Hamilton and anchored out. That evening's sunset beer was a quiet one.

The next morning, I took a slip at the high-end marina in Hamilton, paying $66 for the night. That's $2 a foot for little LOW KEY. I was doing it for the guest, I told myself. Nicely sidetied to the dock at the private island paradise, I gave the boat a well earned freshwater wash down. Passing by the putrid bathrooms, I moseyed into town to shower in the better kept facilities opposite Sunsail.

Tony arrived at the boat and we went to lunch. Tony was not a big drinker. Actually, besides tea, he did not drink at all. That night, I lit the very cool lantern onboard and let Tony acquaint himself with the boat and a good book, while I wandered into "town" to see about the music that filled the marina. I found the source—it was a tourist spot that seemed a little lame. On my way back to the boat, I heard other, better music coming from up in the hill somewhere. I found a road that went straight up into the blackness of the jungle. I took it. Like Odysseus to the Sirens, I was drawn to the musical beat and cacophony of mingling voices. After sneaking along behind the island workers' housing project, I found the place. They called it the "Sports Bar" and it was filled with young itinerants and their drinking friends. Daddy's home, Baby. After a few brews with some fellow travelers, I searched out and found the foot passage back down to the main street. It was a steep winding pathway that plunged down through the foliage, arriving at a dimly lit staircase on the side of a restaurant, slipping me quietly onto the street. Secret entrance—very cool!

Back at the boat, Tony was happily reading, so I walked the dock and met a guy on a little yellow sailboat. I was drawn to his boat because of the aft seating arrangement. He had run a couple of 2x6 boards across the back of the cockpit and attached them onto the middle rungs of the stern pulpit. This made a bench of sorts. Above was a high set bimini. From the "perch" you could see the whole horizon. It was brilliant. We had a couple of beers. This beautiful girl walked up to us, fresh from the shower. She was an incredible half-Maori Kiwi, with burning blue eyes. She instantly qualified to be in the running for my future ex-wife position (we all grieve in different ways). That is until he called out, "Hi honey." We partied into the night.

Tony had a boat parked in a slip in front of his house. He and his mates sailed the bay often. He had been considering whether longer range cruising was for him. On this cruise he wanted to see as much as possible, starting with the islands to the south. I obliged, knowing that the wind was coming from the south. We beat for a couple of hours before he agreed that we could try an easterly course. We beam reached to beautiful Whitehaven Beach. White powder sand and bikini covered, the landfall put me in good spirits. We dropped the main hook and then took the stern anchor to the beach to winch up, just a little bit closer.

After Whitehaven, we cruised up to Hook Island where the snorkeling was supposed to be phenomenal. They had a slew of two-hour moorings there. For two and a half hours we drifted around the anchorage waiting for a mooring to free up. It wasn't so bad as we were barbecuing steaks, listening to Sara Dashew, and drinking beer/tea. Out of nine boats, zero gave up their mooring. We anchored outside the bay in 50 feet. It was there that I learned that Tony had never seen the cinematic masterpiece and cruiser's cult film *Captain Ron*. I whipped up some popcorn and put in the tape. He loved it . . . of course.

Did someone say beach party?

We motored in light air over to perfect Cid Harbour. I could tell there was something brewing because two of the boats in the anchorage were wearing their colors, all flags onboard hoisted. We poked around in the dinghy until we got invited to the ragin' beach party that evening. It was a great sampling of cruisers from all over the world. Beach games, great food and drink, a bonfire and a sing-along; what more could you ask for?

I think Tony might have been all cruisered out because he offered to set us up for the day over at the South Molle Resort. Niiicccee. There was the long putt contest at 1130, beach soccer at 1400, lap pool with coldies on the side, and, of course, a cheeseburger in paradise. That night was all you can eat Mexican food night. I convinced the "chef" that he could not possibly have a Mexican buffet without salsa. He whipped some up and all was right in the world.

Alas, it was finally time to say goodbye to Tony, a kind and gracious guest. We sailed into Airlie and I dropped him at the Sailing Club. Airlie is a true sailor's paradise. Yes, it is a cheery little town with haul-out yards, chandleries and sailing club, but it is also a hub for backpackers, which means the pubs are filled with nubile travelerettes indulging in frothy beverages and trying to get you to take them sailing in the Whitsundays.

That night I went out with Phil and his son Ray. Young Ray just got back from serving in the Gulf. He has had his picture in the Underway section of *Lats & Atts* twice. We did Airlie right, hitting every bar, pub and club. Ray and I got on the tequila early. The night ended in the wee hours with Phil finding Ray passed out on the sidewalk and me awol. Doing my best Lost in Space robot impression, I had switched into automatic "return-to-boat" mode and somehow managed to do just that.

Boatyard fun

The boatyard told me that at high tide the water would be plenty deep enough to get me up the creek to the ways where the travelift could snatch me up before the water receded. I did not even make it to the first channel marker before furrowing into the mud. Still, the tide was rising and so I continued to push LOW KEY further up the bank thinking it would drop off at some point. As the tide maxed out, I put a call in to the yard and the little boat came out to tow me . . . up the bank further. I soon had visions of a night on my side, which worried me less than the proximity of the mangroves which meant "midgies," a gruesome little insect which make mosquitoes look like baby fur seals. I had them turn the dog and pony show around and get me back into deeper water. I had to wait for the even higher high tide which, of course, was in the middle of the night. I am used to it. Somehow every particularly tricky navigational situation ends up being a night operation onboard LOW KEY. It is not always my fault, it's just the way it is.

So there I was, minding my own business sitting calmly back at anchor, when I felt the urge to venture into the Sailing Club. Of course Phil was there, this time with his friend Tich. With an unending flow of schooners (pints), we settled in for the afternoon. I was geared up and mentally prepared that day to begin a week of torture in the yard and then, suddenly, there I was, fully at rest in a happy place.

After dinn . . . sorry, tea, young Michael joined me on the boat for another try at the creeky haul-out. I let Mike drive while I pointed out the winding way through the mangroves. It was a ridiculous situation. It was dark and the markers went from bright floats to dark sticks in the mud as we ventured deeper into the bush. Some local had told me to stay against the brush on the left. Did he mean his left or mine? Looking over the side, I would have sworn that the water was ankle deep, but there we were doing a knot and a half with a six-foot keel, pushing tree branches out of the way. I finally did miss a marker and directed us into the mud again. Technically, since Mike was driving, one could say that he went aground . . . no? We made it to the lift and they raised us a couple of feet above the water, shut the big blue contraption down, and went home.

CHAPTER 11

On the Hard in Airlie Beach

I was hanging out at the Great Barrier Reef town of Airlie
Beach. Besides being well equipped for servicing sailing, Airlie
hosts some of Australia's vacationing wealthy. With the town's
close proximity to the Whitsunday Islands, it also caters to
backpackers from around the world. An additional draw on
Airlie's roster this year was the upcoming *Latitudes & Attitudes
Cruiser's Bash*—The Plunda down unda).

Sailing from day to day in warm aft breezes, from one perfect island anchorage to the next, enjoying reef snorkels, sundowners and shooting stars, can be a little tiring. I decided to
take a break from it all to haul the boat during my stay in Airlie. Now, normally haul-outs suck, but in this case I did not
have much to complain about. My new best friend Phil, and his
family, had offered to put me up in their home while LOW KEY
was out of the water. This was a windfall for me. Being in a
yard is hard enough with long hours working in a toxic environment, but having to put away your tools each evening to
clear a space in the dust to dine and sleep makes things, well,
lame. Having a clean shower, then a coldy or two on the veranda followed by a nice meal with the family and an evening
in front of the telly, was a much appreciated upgrade.

I had made the treacherous passage up the creek at high tide
the night before and gotten safely into the slings of the Travelift.
Why did they want LOW KEY in the slings? Because at low tide,

the Travelift ways drain completely. At the crack of 1000, we made it down to the boatyard to find LOW KEY sitting happily across the yard in her hardstand and ready to be cleaned up. Phil went right to work with the high pressure washer to clean off what growth there was.

I met with a couple of shipwrights, an American and an Australian, about my rudder issues. When the boat would surf, the rudder would shimmy back and forth. It was more funny than disconcerting but still, it was something that I wanted to fix. It was loose at the very bottom where it connected to the skeg and it was also loose where the stainless post ran up through the fiberglass shaft in the boat. There were no bearings and so, after 32 years, the stainless had worn back some of the fiberglass allowing some play. The shipwrights had all kinds of plans for me, some I did not agree with. Still, I could not do all of the work myself and time was money and all of that, so I let them take the rudder to repair the base. How much trouble could they get into?

We went to work on the waterline. It needed to be painted, but there were a couple of blisters. I told Phil that I was going to wait until Venezuela, where the slave labor is cheap, to have them fixed. Phil had brought down a bunch of his tools and lying right there was a new, in the box, grinder. I could not help myself. I bolted on one of my sanding disks, suited up and went to work. By the time I was done, I had made a pretty big mess. It was good to get in and do it right. My assistant learned how to fill the gaps while I gave the bottom paint a quick going over with the sander. I nearly lost my helper when Frank, the funny chandlery guy and boatyard guru, walked by and joked with Phil that Woody needed a little practice with the putty knife. Phil had done a good job; I really could not complain. I felt I was getting my money's worth.

After a couple of days, my rudder returned. The guys had ground back the glass, welded in a piece of steel, and filled it back up. Somehow it came to over $400 (including a consultation fee). It was almost as much as the haul out. I could have paid a welder $60 and done the rest myself. I sucked it up, smiled, and paid them.

My spendy shipwrongs had recommended a couple of things to tighten up the rudder in the shaft, none of which would have withstood the thrashing of another ocean crossing. I decided to fix it with a process that we use on smaller racing boats back home. We waxed the rudder post and put it back into the boat. We jammed clay up into the small gap between the post and the hull. We then drilled holes in the shaft and injected an epoxy/graphite mixture into it and went home for the night. In the back of my mind was the ominous concern that the epoxy would get through the wax and adhere to the rudder post. Then I would have to cut off the back of the boat to get the rudder out.

The next morning, we came down and used one of the big steel boat supports lying in the yard to break loose the rudder post from the shaft. It came free but was pretty tight. I could have used more graphite and given it more time to fully cure—it had been chilly that night. The next day, the epoxy had completely set up and the rudder came out. I spent a couple of hours with sandpaper wrapped around some exhaust hose, sanding back some of my new black epoxy. Eventually . . . it came out better than new!

In trouble with the law . . .

Customs had finally tracked me down. They came by the yard to interrogate me. I was supposed to check in at each stop with Customs. To save myself some time finding and visiting each Customs office, I had been calling their 1-800 number and reporting in on their message machine. The guy seemed a little edgy. He explained that I should be going into each office when I arrive somewhere. Stupid, but O.K. But that was not why he drove 50 kilometers from Mackay to find me. He explained how I had violated my visa requirements by cruising on an invalid cruising permit. Not me, I thought, I'm pretty careful with paperwork. He was sure, though, and went on to explain how much trouble I was in. I showed him my cruising permit.

"Someone had messed up in Sydney," he explained, and then he almost apologized. In the end, he gave me some good tips about cruising north and for dealing with Customs.

Right after Customs left, a cute young reporter named Julia came by to interview me. She was from one of the newspapers that Phil had enlisted to help promote the *Latitudes & Attitudes Cruiser's Bash*. I don't think she was very impressed with the boat. It was not LOW KEY's fault. Boats never look good when you first haul them. She got her story and pictures, and before I could offer her a frosty beverage, she rushed off to cover a plane crash. First time I'd heard that one.

Bill and David Edge, a father and son team, own Edge's Boatyard in Airlie Beach, Queensland. Great guys, nice yard, good price, etc. If you have ever hauled your boat, then you probably know what a Travelift is. For those who do not, it is a massive blue steel framework on wheels that picks up boats and drives them around. These guys were having trouble getting one for their yard, so Dave just built his own—a 40-ton version. How cool is that?

Did someone say . . . party?

Phil is a big fan of *Lats & Atts*. He was the one that had organized Australia's first *Latitudes & Attitudes Cruiser's Bash*. By the time all was said and done, Phil had secured for us use of the Whitsunday Sailing Club, a special cruiser-priced buffet, an entertainer, as well as free promotion on the local radio stations and newspapers. He and his family handed out hundreds of flyers at the local boating retailers and the boatshow. He had tried to plan it around Bob's schedule—ya right. It was not until about a week before the event that Bob found the time that allowed him and Jody to make it. This was great news!

On the morning that Bob and Jody were coming in, I arrived at the yard to find the cruising sloop PANDEMONIUM next to me in a boat stand. My friend Dave, and his lovely Danish cruising partner Phillipa (whom the cruisers had renamed

Flippa since our last encounter), had arrived on the night tide. They were just in time for the party. I had intended to meet Bob and Jody at the airport, but boatyard duties called. Phil brought them by the yard to say hello. It was great to see them. They are family to me and it had been over a year since I had seen them back in California. They met Dave and Flippa, and that evening we all met back at Phil and Sue's for a great night of catching up and other lively cruising conversation.

Late that night, Dena, my recently former cruising companion, swept through town. When she left LOW KEY a month before, she had joined another boat that headed north and explored all of the islands and beautiful reef anchorages up to the city of Cairns (say Cans). She decided that she did not like that boat so much (having been mostly spoiled on LOW KEY?), and so she came back down to Airlie to see if I might give her a lift to Darwin to complete her Australian tour. Her timing was pretty good. When finally leaving Airlie, LOW KEY would have to make tracks and skip most of the cool stuff that she had gotten to see while on the other boat.

She missed the charter week and a week in the yard. But fortunately for her, she arrived on the morning of the big party. Coincidence? Maybe. Wily, I say. Still, it was great to see her.

She would, over the next couple of days, remind me of the valuable services she could provide for our trip to Darwin. You know, provisioning and cooking and stuff. My notices around town had supplied some promising leads for crew. I was leaning towards the three German girls. I chose Dena in the end.

Was it Saturday already? It was the big day of the Party. Dave, Flippa, Dena and I went down to the boatshow at the marina early that evening to party on a big 100-year-old schooner. We grabbed a couple revelers from there and headed up to the *Lats*' party. It was early and it was already ragin'. We added our pitchers to the pitchers on Phil's table and the four of us started in with the tattooing. *Lats* makes temporary tattoos, one with a nice nautical design and the other with our mascot, Atty. Flippa and Dena did the guys and Dave and I got on the women, applying tattoos. Later that night, we had a loudest Hawaiian shirt contest. My favorite was Phil's friend, Tich, who had a matching Hawaiian shirt and tie combo. We finally chose the guy with a bright shirt and blinding, non-matching shorts. Tasty food, good music and great company—Plunda down undah success.

CHAPTER 12

Purgatory

We had survived the first Australian *Latitudes & Attitudes Cruisers' Party* coupled with a visit from Bob and Jody. Still in Airlie Beach on the Barrier Reef in Australia, LOW KEY was hauled out and parked next to friends Dave and Flippa on PANDEMONIUM. Dena had returned for a lift north to Darwin.

After hauling, inspection of the hull revealed a small crack at the aft end of the keel to hull joint. People are always saying that boats are a trade off. Here was a good example. In order to make the Cal 33 faster, the designer, or possibly the builder, shaped the aft end of the keel into a sharp edge. Well sharp edges, fiberglass and high loads do not mix. When they set the boat down, the edge cracked and compressed into itself.

Grinder in hand, I went at it and got back to clean fiberglass and ground back a foot or so on all sides. I then laid up some glass with epoxy, sanded that smooth and slapped on some two-part sealing primer. By the time I was done, my friend Phil had finished the bottom painting and we were ready to go back into the water. The Travelift was brought around and lifted LOW KEY from her blocks. I heard the crunch. I was kinda hoping it had come from another part of the yard. I looked under the boat and saw that my freshly painted keel patch had ripped out. I had glassed it up while the boat was compressed. Of course, when the boat was lifted, the keel went back to its normal position, taking my patch with it. It was a rookie move; I

just hadn't thought it all the way through. Bill from the yard
wanted to set it down right away before the keel fell off. I was
pretty sure that was not going to happen but, if it was, I wanted
it to happen there in the yard and not in the middle of some
cold ocean. I pondered the situation and, duty bound, took pictures. I was tired and beaten. We raised up the aft jack stands
and set the boat back down, this time leaving the aft end of the
keel hanging in case I decided to fix it right instead of checking
airfares. I think Phil saw it in my eyes, defeat creeping in. He
convinced me to take the rest of the afternoon off.

I returned to the yard the next day, rested and determined.
Back into my gear, I went and I started grinding away at my
freshly ripped-out fiberglass patch. I ended up going through the
glass where the aft end of the keel met the hull. Yep, I thought,
looking through the hole, that's the inside of the bilge alright.
Monday arrived and the local boatworker guys came around to
see the trouble that the 'seppo' (septic tank yank) had gotten
into. One of them was a shipwright named Sean. He was a fiber-
glassing expert who reminded me of the surfboard shapers back
home. He went right to work explaining "the fix," going so far
as etching lines in the new bottom paint to show how far back
I needed to grind and glass up to "make it right."

I try to do my own work, mostly to save money, but also to
learn. If I do not know how to do something, then I will have
someone show me. But you also need to know when you are in
over your head. This was an important, life preserving boat
issue that needed to be done right. I hired Sean to help me. I
told him that I would do all of the slave labor to keep his time
invested down. We did not even talk money, he was just one of
those guys I knew I could trust to give me a good deal. Asking
Sean to do the work caused some problems with the guys who
overcharged me for working on my rudder. They expected to
get the job. They weren't in the running.

While in the yard, I met Jo and her husband Steve, who
were there working on their cruising catamaran. Jo writes for
all kinds of sailing magazines and has even lowered herself to
do an article for *Latitudes & Attitudes* now and again. With

Dena, Steve and Jo and my friends Dave and Flippa all in the yard, it was hard not to do a little evening socializing. At night we would cook our meals in the boats and then bring them down to the "concession" area and share in good food, boxed wine, and cruising tales.

Turns out that Steve and Jo had an extra car that they were trying to get rid of. They told us to, "Take it, use up the gas before it goes to the junk yard. If it breaks down just leave it." It was a nice little car! We were mobile. It was great to be able to drive around, especially when trying to escape the yard to run "errands."

In the dirty, dusty, tired environment of a boatyard, you must let go of some of your expectations of normalcy. Dena pointed out the strange boatyard behavior of some of the guys. She was in the outdoor kitchen area when she spotted Dave drying his freshly washed dishes with the shirt he was wearing. While washing her own dishes, she noticed white powder flying about and getting all over. Steve was mixing a batch of epoxy and filler on the picnic table behind her. "It's a boatyard," I tried to explain. Later, Dave found himself falling into the boatyard lull of working for four minutes and then shooting the bull with fellow inmates for fifteen. I warned him that some of these people had been in here for over a year. Like the dinosaurs at La Brea Tar Pits, he was slowly being sucked down into the gooey abyss that could enslave him in boatyard hell forever.

And then came the big day. I had ground back to bare glass on a very wide area under the boat and around the old patch area. Sean assembled all of the stuff we would need and we went to work, glassing up the bottom. We worked fast. I learned a lot that day. By the end of the afternoon, we had built up the glass much thicker than the original layup. The next two days were spent grinding, filling, grinding, sanding, filling, sanding and priming. I had some spare time waiting for the new section to cure, so after 9,000 miles of sailing without it, I installed the compass. I don't know what all of the fuss was about. I still barely use it. It's good for a backup, I suppose.

I was scheduled to try again to get back into the water the

following day. It was Friday so I knocked off early to join all the boatyard guys (Dena was already there) over in the corner where we told bad jokes and drank the *eskie* dry.

The next day they picked up LOW KEY again and this time there was no crunch. The industrial strength rebuild held. I could see, though, how lightweight the boat really was. When they picked her up, the keel moved. I could move it by hand, side to side about an inch, and see the hull flex forward and aft of the keel. I was starting to understand why some people look surprised when I tell them I am trying to circumnavigate in a coastal boat like a Cal. I have since gotten a lot of feedback from Cal "experts" and have decided to continue on with my cruise.

Freedom

The tide would not be in until 10:00 pm so David, the yard owner, hung LOW KEY low over the empty ways. He explained that the tide would come in and lift the boat, that's when I'll know that there is enough water in the creek to get out. Classic. It all went to plan until I fired her up. The engine sounded funny—no cooling water. I was not spending another day in the yard. I went right up the line: the valve was on, there was water at the filter, water after the pump, water at the front of the engine, but nothing where the water joined the exhaust. I started getting the tools out to dismantle the thermostat which was nicely sealed up and for which I would have to build a new gasket to reassemble it. Phil looked in. "Did you try a hammer?" followed by, "Works on submarines!" The mystery as to why the U.S. only sends diesel subs and not nuclear ones down under had been solved. I tried the hammer, tapping the thermostat and the water jacket. It worked.

In the moonless night we quietly made our way back down the jungle ride at Disneyland, followed by the half mile section that dries at low tide and escaped into the deeper comfort of the Bay. Sooo sweet to be back at anchor with a nice breeze and the easy motion of the boat back in her element.

The last few days of our visit to Airlie were spent provisioning and readying the boat by day. At night we hung out with friends. We went to Sean's house for dinner and a movie. It turns out that our glasser, Sean, was also a great cook and artist who does amazing sculptures. I made pizza for Phil's family. We took a night to party with everyone at the Sailing Club. Dena and I spent the last night quietly, in the palatial guest accommodations at Phil and Sue's place, languishing in a big four-sided bed, TV on in the corner . . . a vacation from our vacation.

Of course I tried to get Phil to join us on the leg up the coast to Cairns, but he had other guests coming. How do you thank people that have done so much for you? I'll start by saying, Thanks, you guys!

North to Lizard

I pulled up the anchor and we drifted out of Muddy Bay. It had been a long time since we were at sea going anywhere. It was good to be free of land again. I was in such a good mood that I didn't even cringe when Dena put on her favorite cruising CD from songstress Eileen Quinn. We sailed up and around a corner, arriving at Monty's Resort for sunset. After our arrival coldy, we ventured ashore. Monty's was not the happenin' spot that night. We walked down the beach and found the very plush Cape Gloucester Eco-Resort. The place was cruiser friendly. They had beautiful showers for the yachties and a great open dining area with big screen. We had a couple of jugs of beer and talked to Murray, the manager.

The good thing about parking at night is that you do not know until morning (if you're lucky) that you parked near a big coral head. The good thing about waiting to re-anchor the next evening is that you do not know until morning (if you're luckier still) that you re-parked among many coral heads.

We sailed north. It was the first night sail we had enjoyed in a month. I came off watch and as I lay down to sleep, I was aware of all of the noise in my head—all of the thoughts and petty concerns that had piled up while shorebound. I knew that a day or two at sea would settle my mind and put me back at ease.

We pulled into the big town of Cairns and anchored in the river out front. It was one of those places where you have three knots of current running both in and out with the tides. I dropped the hook toward the windward shore and backed into deeper water to set it. The boat turned with the tide, but the arc of the chain on a slope kept us from moving too far.

A lot of the reef-exploring charter boats are based in Cairns. These boats buy a lot of fuel which has made the big fuel dock not so cruiser friendly. We sailed out the bay and around the corner to a place called Yorky's Knob. I know; you wouldn't expect much from a place called Yorky's Knob. But it was great with a beautiful marina, nice yacht club and friendly people, all nestled in amid lush mini mountains. The place was inexpensive with slips for $.50 a foot, free water, and fuel that was cheaper than Cairns (still almost $4 a gallon, as in all of Australia). The fuel dock had easy access and they even let us leave the boat there while we enjoyed what the yacht club had on tap.

When headed north during Australia's winter, you get solid southeast winds. Being inside the world's largest reef, you get the benefit of perfect wind without the swell. We made quick work of the leg to beautiful Lizard Island. A renowned stop for northbound cruisers, Lizard is known for its great anchorage, crystal blue water, white sand beach, and killer lookout hike. Captain Cook himself, after months of unnerving navigation of the inner reefs, hiked to the top of Lizard and spotted a gap in the outer reef that would finally lead his ship to deep water.

That night we were invited to hang out with the rest of the cruising folk on the beach for Bocce Ball, potluck, and a candlelight bonfire. A proper bonfire would have been illegal on protected Lizard, so they lit a big citronella candle and we pretended. The way the conversation and cask wine (Oz-fancy for box wine) flowed, I'm not sure any of us noticed.

Besides my Cal 33, there were two other Cals in the bay. One was a newer Cal 36 (which did not have problems) and the other, an old Cal 39. All three had crossed the not so Pacific. The other cruisers, mostly full keelers, sat back, gratefully removed from frightful stories of hull flex, boat twist and floppy keels.

It was in Lizard that I finally fired up our watermaker. It was a Katadyn PowerSurvivor 40e that I had brought all the way out from California. LOW KEY holds over 50 gallons of water and, so far, we had not needed to make water. The upcoming 6,000-mile sail across the Indian Ocean inspired me to finally finish the installation. I was also concerned because the manual said that the pickling process, to preserve the live membrane, was only good for a year. I flipped the switch and watched as tubes of bubbles and brine ebbed and flowed. After a couple of minutes, there it was: beautiful, clean, fresh water made from the bounty of the sea (and a little wind-generated electricity). What a great little toy.

Next to us was an old yellow ketch. The guy was Australian and had sailed all around his country. Talking to him reminded me that people are cruising on budgets even slighter than ours. He was telling me how, after his refer broke down, he built a new one using parts from discarded refrigerators and a used belt-driven air conditioner compressor from a car. He welded it up himself and the whole system cost him $8. In the real world, being able to work with your hands has high value.

How do porcupines mate?

As the old saying goes, "Very carefully." It was time to get going north. We had over 300 miles to cover to get to the top of Australia. Easy, right? I checked out the charts and found the route to be perilously reef strewn. A more danger-fraught stretch of water I had never seen. I plotted it out on the charts and found that, in some places, we would only be a couple hundred feet from the jagged reefs. I decided that we would not stop like the other boats, but sail on through the nights. I had my top watch girl onboard (who was also an excellent swimmer). Big ships navigate the narrow channels at all hours, why couldn't we? In hindsight, the ship thing should have been an argument to not be out there at night. A big ship in a narrow channel will not turn to avoid you and will not slow down and risk losing steerage, even if he knows he is going to plow over you.

I triple checked my waypoints and off we went. On the GPS, I had plotted not just my course line but had also placed dots on each side that represented the edges of reefs. It occurred to me, in the black of night as I watched the dots on the little GPS screen go by, that it was possible that the charts could be off. I let that thought go. Did I mention we left on a *Friday*? Who can keep track of the days out here?

The good thing about sailing through an endless minefield of reefs is that without fetch, there is no swell. It was an unbelievably beautiful sail. We had 20 to 30 knots always from somewhere aft. From the comfort of the beanbag, a tug of the port string here or the starboard string there kept Nessie steering us down our line. By day we sailed quietly by little sandy cays and small palm islands. By night we counted stars (while keeping the boat dead center on the little GPS line). At first I kept us off the beaten path, thinking we could avoid ships. We only encountered a few. Later I switched our track to run up the side of the shipping lanes so we could make use of the channel lights. Also, I figured that the charts might be more accurate near the shipping lanes. It all worked out—we ran the gauntlet without incident.

Vicious fishes

I hate to admit it, but I do not do a lot of fishing. There is always so much going on, who has got the time? Actually Dena, a vegetarian who would not even eat a fish if caught, was the one who insisted we put a line out (some kind of midwestern fishing gene she can't shake). So I brought him out. I call him "fish killer." He is my lean, mean, green (and yellow) squid-looking lure that, before entering Australian waters, was batting about 500. Suffering a down-under run of 0 for 3, he was due. I pulled him in after sunset to discover that he had been macerated. He was shredded. Even his super hard plastic head had a sizable chunk taken out of it. Now I was pissed.

The next day I put in the lure that Dena had gotten me for my birthday. I thought the guy at the shop was putting her on because it was a huge, deformed, freak lure that rattled when you shook it. We hooked up right away. It was a 3-4 foot . . . somethin', and it was jumping all over the place. Before I could figure out how to slow the boat down, it got off. I pulled in the line to find that it had taken my new birthday lure and that hurt. With a one-for-one record, that special lure was like a bright streaking comet, living a short but illustrious life. The fish had sliced the 80-pound nylon leader. I built a better lure and this time used a steel leader. We hooked up again, an even bigger fish. And again, it got away. That fish had ripped the steel leader line out of its crimp. I had never seen that before. Dena wanted to know what happens to the fish after they take a lure? I could not see through my haze of fury to answer her. It was on. I started building super lures, frightening three-pronged, double-crimped creatures. Alas, before I could get them much sea time, we had arrived at Thursday Island, north of Cape York.

Thursday does not have that great of an anchorage. It is pretty exposed and there is a lot of current sweeping through. We went ashore and found a shower at the rugby field. We checked out the town. It was a cool little place. We found a pub that proclaimed itself to be the Australia's Top Pub. Get it? It was a mandatory jug o' beer stop. We sailed out that same day.

Last leg

We were headed to Darwin just 700 nm away. Finally, some open water. The oppression of the constant vigilance required to keep my soft fiberglass bottom from being torn up on hard sharp reef had ended. The free open water was welcome. It was also a special occasion for another reason. It was finally time to bottle Captain Woody's Private Reserve. I had patiently waited the five days it took to ferment my first batch of beer. My precious 6.07 gallons of brew was very vulnerable while in its primary fermentation stage. It was comforting to finally be able to give it the protection of bottling. So decant I did. Now, I would have to wait another full week to partake of my creation, which would bring us together, make us one!

You know how it is. The sun is setting and you are gleefully sailing along in 15 knots of wind in flat seas, when the wind strength slowly doubles. Through the night the seas build into a cranky, lumpy, steep mess, tossing you to and fro. Dawn comes ("early on a boat, happens every morning, just about sun up"—Capt. Ron) and your patience has been rewarded. The swell has finally found its shape. It is towering now, but its period is longer, making its slope less steep, and the motion of the boat has now returned to friendly.

I have got one of those CARD devices instead of an active radar (a third the cost, 1/50th the energy consumption). It receives radar signals from other boats and beeps accordingly. You get a ping each time the ship's radome comes around. I like to try and spot the ships before the Card does. We were sailing along and the Card started going crazy. It was beeping quickly for a few seconds at a time. I had been keeping a good watch and when I looked around again, I saw nothing. Soon the Card was beeping constantly. Visions of boats that had been wrecked by unseen submarines flooded my mind. I turned the Card off and heard the engines of the plane. It was the Australian Coast Guard. I turned up the radio and suffered another friendly debriefing: Boat name, number of persons onboard, last port, next port, animals, guns, dead bodies, terrorists . . . just seeing if you are paying attention.

And at last, we arrived. After six months of cruising Australia, Darwin would be our last Australian port of call. And there was another last of the adventure. It was the last time that Dena would sail with LOW KEY and me. I was sad to see her go. Peace had eluded us and we had convinced ourselves that the few lows outweighed the many highs. Dena and I spent another day together and then said our goodbyes. It was a hard thing.

CHAPTER 13

Last Stop in Oz

I was anchored off the Darwin Sailing Club in the Northern Territory, Australia. When I say anchored off, I mean anchored way off. In Darwin, you have the choice of anchoring by the industrial downtown area or outside of town, off the plush and amenity-rich Sailing Club. The only problem with the Sailing Club anchorage is that you have to anchor up to a mile out. It is very shallow and there are 20-foot tides. I would set my alarm at night to check the depth at max low to see if I could inch in closer to shore. LOW KEY draws six feet, but during the neap tide I figured I could park amongst the shallow catamarans, just inches above the mud.

I would be in Darwin for three weeks prepping the boat for the Indian Ocean crossing—mostly beefing things up for the notoriously rough southern areas. Being near the club was handy. Along with facilities that you would find in any self-respecting sailing club like cold beer and hot food, the DSC had a reasonably priced, well-stocked chandlery.

Just up the road I attended the 30th Annual Beer Can Regatta, a Northern Territory classic. Teams work hard all year emptying cans of their favorite beverage to have enough material to build a small sea vessel. Surprisingly, most of the boats floated and some were even made to go in a straight line as teams chugged down the contents of next year's building material.

I walked over to Cullen Bay where there is a beautiful marina, restaurant, and entertainment area surrounded by large lakeside homes. I remembered back to when I was crewing on the Royal Yacht of Selangor and we had visited the marina, years before. There were seven upscale restaurants on the waterfront. I remembered making a point of having dinner at every one of them. On this current adventure, however, that kind of indulgence was a foreign concept indeed. I took the scenic route back to the Sailing Club which led me across Mindil Beach. I met some backpacker babes trekking around Australia in an old campervan. Compared to the backpacker economy, I was doing pretty well. I figured that all three groups, from lowly backpacker to high end yachtie, were doing just fine enjoying to the fullest our current slice of life.

About once a week, the whole town of Darwin would shut down for a holiday. What were the occasions? The first was because there was a big horse race over at the track and the second was because the carnival was in town. Everybody likes a day off!

Being a jumping-off point for the Indian Ocean, Darwin gets its share of cruising traffic. After the current slew of regattas had left, the anchorage got really quiet. It was fine at first because I was getting a lot done. But as the job list shortened, I started getting a little lonely in the evenings. I decided to head around to the other anchorage to find some friends. I was on deck preparing to haul the hook when I saw a couple boats on the horizon. They were just arriving. It was PATRON and ALTAIR and a couple others. We all went in for dinner at the club that night.

A few of the worklist items for LOW KEY while visiting fair Darwin: I procured, cut and glassed in the forward bulkhead, changed the oil and filters, refit a couple of deck bolts that were leaking and pulled off the bow pulpit to fill some rot. I spent a lot of time up the rig. I changed out the main halyard and an in-mast fairlead, installed the VHF antennae, ripped out what was left of the wind instruments and masthead lights and all the wiring from inside the mast. Just before I departed Darwin, I found another shroud with a broken wire, so I had two new ones made and I put them up. I stored the still good one as a spare. And I greased the rudder shaft with a gun I borrowed from PATRON. I need to buy my own but am holding out to find this mini one-handed model I borrowed in the boat yard back in Airlie.

I pulled anchor one morning to get a little closer to the club, and as I put it in gear, I heard a loud rattling. I dropped the hook again and hopped into the croc-infested waters, after a long look around. The shaft zinc had loosened. I cranked it tight and cleaned up the prop and shaft and climbed out, surviving the experience unscathed.

I had to shop for sixty days. I found out that a supermarket in Darwin would deliver my shopping to the Sailing Club. Cool. I shopped and took the bus back, and while I waited at the club, I had a couple pitchers with HARMONY (Tika, Bob and Andy) and friends. After a lively game of pool, I trucked my food out to the boat through the chop.

While in Darwin, I looked for crew for the crossing to South Africa. I posted flyers in likely spots where the backpacker set would see them. I got a few bites but did not meet anyone that I wanted to spend every day with for the next three months. I had wanted to someday do an ocean crossing solo. Why not solo the toughest one?

Chasing the sun

And finally, it was departure day. I thought it would never come. I could not wait to be at sea again, where the safety and comfort of the crew was the priority instead of the daily grind of boat work. I get satisfaction from working on the boat, just not in that quantity. I was looking forward to some rest and relaxation.

I went to shore for the last time (you know, the last time for a while, hopefully not the last time ever). I pulled a chair up to the phone at the Sailing Club and made some calls to use up the rest of my Aussie phone card. Back at home, I caught my friends at the end of a beach day. Everyone was there and having a great time as usual playing ball, hanging out and having a couple of coldies. It was good to know that some things never change. For my ceremonial last meal, I had some fries and a coldy of my own. I headed out to the boat and pulled up the hook.

The wind was light to nonexistent that first week, which was unfortunate. With no wind there are no sail adjustments or changes and nothing is breaking. I was left with nothing to do. Being my first time singlehanding, I was horribly bored. Going through a break up of sorts didn't improve my outlook. I had some books onboard that I had been wanting to read for years. I had literally brought them half way around the world. And now I had the time to read them. I would soon discover that there is a limit to the amount of reading that one can do.

I am very fortunate to have as a good friend world famous sailor/writer Tania Aebi. Among her other accomplishments, she sailed around the world solo when she was 18. Before I departed Darwin, I asked her for advice, specifically, about the sleeping situation when singlehanding. She said that I was going to like singlehanding. She said to sleep when I wanted to. If I wake up for some reason, then I should have a look around. She noted that more prudence would be required for crossing traffic lanes and when near land. I am a fan of sleep. I was glad to learn that I would not be missing any. She also said that the first few days might be hard, but that I would get used to being alone and even like it. She was right, of course.

LOW KEY holds about four days of fuel, meaning we can motor for four days. But with 6,000 miles to the next affordable fuel, what's the point? Still, for entertainment and to feel like some progress was being made, I started motoring during the day. At some point in the evening, I would shut everything down except the VHF, CARD, and nav lights, and just go to sleep. Most of the time I was in a flat calm sea. It was like parking a car in the middle of a vast empty parking lot that stretches to the horizon on all sides. I would wake up a little while later, a little ways down current, have a look around and go back to sleep. It is amazing what gathers around a boat when parked in the middle of a flat sea. I'm told it is the shade and the protection of the hull that the critters are attracted to. I saw turtles of course, but I also saw Australian sea snakes. Big seven-foot serpents just basking on the surface. They seemed so out of place in the ocean.

My fifth day out was a beautiful blue sky day. The water was amazingly clear. I would not have been able to judge the depths if my new friends had not come to visit me. I could see them a hundred feet down, their sharp tails shifting side to side, cutting cleanly through the water as they circled up to inspect me. They were blue sharks, and they looked hungry. I sat on the rail for a while, my feet just above the water. I opened a canned ham for lunch and tried to share it with them, but they were not interested. Seeing them up close like that, in their deep water environment, was a lucky experience that I will never forget.

I have my Aries wind steering system and it works great—when there is wind. While motoring through dead calms, I was reduced to hand steering. It was not as bad as it sounds. I would tie the tiller up and make adjustments every few minutes. I broke out the electric tiller pilot that I bought used in Australia for just this kind of occasion. I pulled it apart and cleaned it up and rigged a mounting system. I put everything together and fired it up. It ran for about four seconds. I traced the problem back to the circuit board. Well out of my technical bounds, I went back to hand steering.

While in Darwin, I installed the old VHF that the boat LAST PENNY had donated to my cause. I think they had meant to lend it to me, but I have not seen them since. It is great to have a working VHF. I am safer at sea and chatty anchorages are so much more fun now. Before Darwin, I only had a handheld VHF. It was a good one! I bought the best. I bought the new miniature waterproof one from Standard. It never worked right. The barometer accessory never worked and the squelch would malfunction every 20 minutes, breaking up peaceful sailing with unstoppable static. We tried to get used to it. Sometimes we would turn the volume down and forget that we had. With ships bearing down and unable to contact us, it could create an unsafe situation. I e-mailed them and they responded right away. They told me to read the manual. Nice. Like I hadn't thought of that. For that matter, my Standard depth sounder has never worked right—new out of the box. The sounder is the only gauge I have in the cockpit, the only gauge that is important to me. They wouldn't let me exchange it at the dealer in Oz. They said I could send it back to California for repair, but it wasn't something that I could live without, literally.

I make a point to not "work" much on passages, but I needed the distraction. It was so calm, I did laundry and dried it in the rigging. I started primary fermentation on another brew, just in case. I did some work on the SSB to increase performance (isolating the antennae lead and expanding ground plane). I finished up my big bean bag! I had worn the old one out on the Pacific crossing and the little one just wasn't cutting it. We had taken the old one apart and used the panels to shape new ones from marine vinyl. I had finally finished the mile of sewing. I forgot how incredibly comfortable the bean bag makes sailing. Also, I pulled out LOW KEY's spare tiller to make sure it fit. My coastal boat did not come with a spare, so I bought a wheel barrel handle from the hardware store. The check-out guy asked me, "Ain't ja gonna replace 'em both?"

There are a couple of good things about motoring. It's true! While motoring, electricity was more plentiful. I could run the watermaker and refer for as long I wanted. Besides full water tanks I had to live with frost on the side of my sunset coldies.

And finally, the wind filled in. With sails drawing full and the boat steering herself, we were finally making fast easy progress toward our next encounter with paradise.

Pirates

The boat was sailing well, in a nice breeze off the wind. We were in the groove. I was below whipping up lunch when I heard engines close by. I threw on some shorts and popped out on deck in time to see two homemade Indonesian boats passing close to starboard, each cluttered with guys. They were hilarious boats—forty-plus feet with a long pointy bow and a square stern being pushed onto plane by slow turning diesels. Above the gunwales they looked like house boats made out of plywood and brightly painted. The house filled the boat from bow to stern, and by the way the boats jumped around, I would guess they weren't built for the rigors of the ocean. But here they were, 400 miles from Indonesia. And then I noticed that a few of the guys were wearing black ski masks. It was 85-degrees out. As is customary when abeam of a fellow boater, I found myself waving . . . to the pirates. It was just an old habit that surfaced at an odd time. The guys went from grim, straight-faced contemplation to enthusiastic grinning, waving and smiling. As they passed, a guy on the stern of the last boat was making circular motions and pointing at my wind generator and laughing it up. I looked up, pointed and smiled, and he waved, and so we were friends. They never slowed down. They just zipped off to windward, hopping along over the swells.

I was 500 miles out from Australia. I had not seen anyone for days. The encounter was an unexpected flurry of images and interaction. I considered the vulnerability of being out this far and heading out further still. I had lots of stuff that I am sure they would consider valuable. For a half a second, I was glad that there were no women on board. Alone, I would probably just get shot, or maybe . . . they would sink the boat and take me hostage and eventually I would become an Indo pirate! I could "work" my way up to my own plywood houseboat. Of course I would only steal from the rich (environmentally-unfriendly mega-yachts and maybe a jet skier now and then) and give to the poor (people of my village).

The wind continued to build, and with big winds come big seas that would occasionally join me in the cockpit, but was I complaining? It was much better than being becalmed. When I left Darwin, I spent most of my time in the cockpit, even sleeping there. But I found I could do just as good a watch from the comfort of my leeward settee. The pilothouse watch system: every now and then I would hop up and stand on the first step of the companionway to scan the horizon from the comfort of the dodger. I brought Nessie's adjustment lines forward so I could steer from my lookout spot as well. Down below, snug in my settee bunk, by day I read.

At one point I was reading one of those great Patrick O'Brian books. He was vividly describing a sinking tall ship running fast downwind under too much sail as the crew tried desperately to make landfall before the big ship assumed its watery grave. I laid back and listened to my own vessel charging down swells, water rushing by the hull, little LOW KEY approaching, at full speed, a small spit of an island in the middle of a vast sea. I drifted off.

I had not tried to get weather reports and I had been putting off checking in with the Downwind SSB net. I kind of liked not knowing what was going to happen the next day and not having anyone know where I was. But soon it seemed realistic that I would actually arrive in Cocos at some point, and so I decided to check in and get some entry info. I talked to Mary on TRANQUILITY. They were sitting in the anchorage at Cocos and were saying really nice things about the place. I could not wait to get in and check it out. She gave me an update on the tropical depression plowing its way down from the north and . . . I could not wait to get in, period.

Twenty miles outside of Cocos, I passed my halfway point. I had figured my total mileage for a circumnavigation on my route at 27,277. I was 13,638.5 miles from home in either direction. I would save the celebrating for my island paradise landfall. On final approach to Cocos, I commenced my arrival preparations. I pumped the bilge, emptied the (non-plastic) trash, prepped the bow for anchoring, and put a call in to Customs on the VHF. Customs was asleep, so Rick on TRANQUILITY got on the radio and welcomed me and gave me the details on the entrance to the atoll.

Two-thousand nautical miles in 20 days. I know, I know, it was no record. You always assume that worst case, you will do

100 miles a day, but rarely do you have to endure such a passage, especially on a tradewind route. LOW KEY and I did fine considering we were mostly parked for the first week.

LOW KEY likes to arrive at night, and Cocos was no exception. The entrance was wide and there were good leading lights. I had plotted a route to the anchorage from my e-charts that I did not have a lot of faith in. I decided to park the boat just inside the entrance. It was a little bumpy, but I was not bothered by it and slept like a baby.

Bright and early, I cruised out on deck to find a perfect turquoise anchorage off the bow and Gilligan's Island off to port. Rick came out in his dinghy to lead me around the coral *bommies* and into the anchorage. It really was not necessary considering the unbelievably clear water. Rick and Mary invited me onboard for breakfast. It was much appreciated. Just after breakfast, the German cruising boat STELLA MARIS poked her head around the entrance. STELLA MARIS had no engine, so Rick and I shot out to guide them in, pushing her the last few meters to her parking spot.

That first day was a long one. After cleaning up the boat and returning LOW KEY to her more comfort oriented at-anchor mode, I was ready for my shower. I figured I would pre-shower in the water and have a look to see how my keel was doing while I was at it. I donned my mask and fins and jumped into the water. Sharks! Cool little four-foot blacktips. Kind of aggressive too, gliding up to me and then cutting sharply away. I assumed that their behavior was from someone feeding them. The keel seemed happy too.

You know how it is, after a long passage, settling into a beautiful place. Having cleaned up the boat and showered, sitting in the cockpit of your vessel that has carried you through thick and thin, feeling the satisfaction of your accomplishment, sipping your favorite beverage as the sun settles in for the night. It is a powerful form of elation. And it is my drug of choice.

CHAPTER 14

Cruiser Paradise

People ask me where my favorite sailing destination is. I end up giving them a short list of favorite spots. The top spot shifts with my mood and what part of my sailing adventures I am craving to relive that day. More often than not, the top spot goes to Cocos Keeling. Cocos is the end-all of island paradises for me. About a third of the way across the Indian Ocean, Cocos is an atoll, a large circle of islands sitting in the middle of nowhere. It is what remains from some ancient volcano that blasted its way up from the sea floor only to go dormant and recede back down leaving a ring of coral islands. It is in the perfect spot to break up the cruise from Indo or Oz, to Chagos or Mauritius.

Cocos is the epitome of cruising paradise. It's like someone sat down and designed the perfect cruiser pitstop. The "cruiser's island" is called Direction Island. Beautiful? Yes. The island is one of those white sand, palm tree lined setups bent into a new moon shape to provide protection for the perfect anchorage—ten feet deep of crystal clear blue water over anchor-sticky white sand—ideal conditions for general bliss and a good night sleep. Off to starboard is a pass with a four-knot current which makes for a world class drift dive/snorkel, complete with friendly black tips.

Customs? Easy. I called them on the radio and they told me I could anchor amongst the other yachts. There was no "new arrival" exile. The next morning, a couple of other newcomers and I met the Customs guy on the beach for a casual check-in. After

Customs had cleared me, I took a stroll around my new island. I took a path that led to the windward side. The big, mid-ocean swell was there, relentlessly pounding the reef. I was reminded of the day before when I was out sailing amid the havoc and fury of that same sea. I was suddenly very appreciative of this little speck of an island for providing LOW KEY and me with such a supernal place to languish. I took more pathways to other parts of the island. All around I found little decks and rain shelters built by island gnomes, as far as I knew, to make my stay more enjoyable.

Back at the beautiful beach along the anchorage was the harbor hangout. There was a bigger shelter, just a roof really, which covered two large picnic tables. Tucked up under the roof, cruisers from all over had hung their flags and burgees next to flotsam and jetsam all marked up with info on boats, crews and cruises. It was a history book of the little islands cruising guests. The roof was designed to catch rain water. It did a good job because, when I was there, the two giant water tanks were full. Free, clean, easily accessible rainwater? Sweeet! Bolted next to one of the tanks was one of those hand-cranked rolling laundry squeezers. I had never used one. It cut the drying time in half. And of course there were lines strung between the coconut palms for drying. My dry clothes smelled like paradise.

What is that box hung over there on the roof support? Oh, that's a telephone. It beams a signal via radio to one of the inhabited islands over the horizon. Calls were free to the other islands, and I found that my Australian phone card worked for overseas calls, no extra charge. Do you think any of my friends believed me when I described where I was calling from? Most of them aren't sailors and don't even read *Latitudes & Attitudes* (God forbid). It is their theory that I moved to a trailer park somewhere in the midwest, and have a wife, kids, and an overactive imagination.

And the list of the little island's facilities goes on! There were composting outhouses, a volleyball court, a fixed coconut opener, a hammock, three BBQs for use with wood, briquettes or gas, and barely a bug around. Back at the boat I discovered a really good FM radio station with no commercials—did I tell you the place was paradise?

While no one lives on Direction Island, there were a couple inhabited islands like Home Island and West Island. On Saturday a ferry came to our island to drop off tourists for the day and take cruisers to town. The other islands had a bank, post office, Internet, a bakery and some little stores. You could get propane and fuel, duty free beer and booze and even weather from the Met Shack. It sounded like you had to time stuff just right because with the small population, one guy would close a store to go open another. But I wouldn't know since I couldn't tear myself away from my island.

There were a bunch of cruising boats in the anchorage when I arrived. These were the real deal. Yes, they had made the 9,000nm Pacific crossing but then, instead of turning around or selling out like so many others, these cruisers pointed their bows west again to venture into the less traveled and more treacherous Indian Ocean. And as I usually find on the path less traveled, we had some characters. Every night at five, most of us putted or rowed ashore for a sundowner. I never knew what to expect. I thought I was the man when I brought ashore and shared some boat-brewed LOW KEY Lager. Not so with this crowd; there were a couple of other boats that brewed too. Many in this eclectic group played instruments from guitars to spoons to an accordion. On one of the nights, Rick on TRANQUILITY set up the TV/DVD under the shelter and put on a movie night for all of the cruisers. The feature was *Captain Ron*, of course. On another night, the moon was full and directly above. A coldy and I were lounging in my cockpit beanbag when I spotted it. The moon was so bright and the water so clear that the boat across the way cast a shadow on the powder white sand below her. The place was magical.

$On\ a\ serious\ note$ . . .

___

I joke around a lot, but bad things can happen out here, like anywhere else. I was listening in on the Downwind net for the Indian Ocean that Mary on TRANQUILITY was running. A boat called CARE FREE checked in. Bob and Sue had started their circumnavigation from South Africa. They were 200 miles out of Rodriguez, just 2,200 miles from returning home, when tragedy struck. Sue had come up for watch and could not wake Bob. He had died from a heart attack.

Mary contacted Cocos Customs who contacted Perth Customs who called Mauritius who arranged for an aircraft fly-over at first light. Mary arranged to check with Sue periodically on the SSB through the night and the next day. She also went ashore and used the phone to call Sue's son.

Sue had trouble getting the mainsail down and was not sure that the waypoints programmed into the GPS would lead her safely into Rodriguez. Rodriguez sent their giant supply boat out to her to tow her in. The tow, through the big seas, was successful, and they arrived safely at Rodriguez where Sue's son had flown in to meet her. I felt glad to have someone like Mary looking after us. And Sue, our hearts go out to you!

The longest reach

And too soon, it was time to leave. I said goodbye to new friends and old, pulled up the hook and drifted out the pass. It was blowing 20 knots and my angle of attack was slightly upwind. While in Cocos I had rigged blocks for my new mini headsail. I hoisted that and triple reefed the main and shot down the lee of the atoll. Once clear of the island's protection, the seas came rolling in and I cracked off to starboard and onto the beam reach course to Rodriguez, just 1,983 miles away.

And here is one of the reasons that this particular route is not so popular: It is a little off a beam reach most of the way in winds that average about 20 knots. This can make it a little bumpy. I took a big "welcome to the southern ocean" wave that first night. It caught me off guard, and I experienced a rare discomfort creep through me. When running with the wind, the odd breaking wave will make it into your cockpit, if it's lucky. On a beam reach, and with the shear size of the swells coming up from the southern ocean, the breakers are able to both fill the cockpit and also cover the rest of the boat with whitewater.

A first for LOW KEY, this wave found its way under the companionway sliding hatch and flooded the tracks. With the help of the heeled boat, it poured in onto me in my cozy settee bunk. I do not like salt in the boat—this was record salt. I threw the wet stuff in a bin, wet toweled the salt off cushions and me, stuffed towels under the hatch and set up camp on the floor while the cushions dried. I could have eased off the wind a bit to lessen the impact of the waves, but I had heard on the net that other boats were having trouble getting far enough south on this trip. I had just paid for my southing and was not willing to give any of it up.

We had left at night, LOW KEY and I, and so I had a hard time imagining the state of the ocean that could cause such large breaking waves. As I peaked out at first light, the conditions were revealed. The wind was whipping up white foam. The seas were big and grey, sometimes peaking above LOW KEY's 48-foot rig. Fortunately for us, the period was long which means there was a long ways between swells. This keeps the breakers to a minimum. Standing on deck, I could see them on the horizon. A swell's peak would get too tall and heavy and break off, causing an avalanche of water to tumble down its face. A couple hundred yards later the breaker would die out. I spent most of my time below, though, blissfully reading, eating and sleeping. About once a day the odds would catch up with me, and I would get to experience one of these monsters first hand. It would start with a low, far off rumble. The sound would grow to a roar as the breaker closed with my little boat. I would brace myself for impact out of instinct more than need. As the wave rolled over LOW KEY, the lights would go out.

The first time it happened I thought it was a freak rogue wave and wouldn't happen again. After the second time, I had to consider the odds of my thin coastal boat surviving two weeks of being pummeled by giant breakers. There was a moment of sunlight in my dark ponderings when I realized that I was no longer responsible for another human life. It was only my own life that was at risk now because of my adventurous scheming. It was a comforting thought that would stay with me for the rest of the ocean crossing.

I was finally on deck to experience a boat covering breaker. I was standing on the cockpit seats, steadying myself with a hand on the backstay, when I heard the far off rumble. Somehow it was much less ominous being outside and under the warm sunlight. I watched the breaker bear down on us. It was surreal. LOW KEY and I did nothing. She seemed ambivalent while I stood powerless. We had survived this inconvenience a few times now, and I was hoping for a repeat performance. The big breaker didn't even slow down as it rolled across the decks of little brave LOW KEY. She barely heeled with the force of the impact. The water washed warm over my bare feet and filled the cockpit. The wave swallowed up LOW KEY and then continued past without slowing down. The water covered the entire boat, leaving only the mast and the dodger visible. LOW KEY crouched down under the weight of the water and slowed from six knots to less than four. She continued to plow along underneath the heavy load. It didn't take her long to shake off the water after which she rose up and accelerated to her former pace. Throughout the event, Nessie held her course, unimpressed by the watery onslaught.

It's lucky if you get to experience an event like this so your boat can show you what it's made of. Conditions that seem violent to us usually go unnoticed by our boats. If your boat is built for the sea then there's no need to worry about her. You may be better served allaying the fears in your own head. I learned to enjoy the submarining.

You want to find leaks in your boat? Submerge it under breaking waves. I found a couple small drips where the sheet track was bolted to the rail. I have a strict no leak policy aboard LOW KEY. I turned off the wind (just for a minute!) and caulk gunned around the rail.

About the middle of the trip, the wind went slightly aft and I was able to crack off a little. I took the main down to give the headsail more air and the helm more control (LOW KEY prefers it that way), and the ride smoothed out. The odd breaker was no longer able to get aboard. The white water would come crashing down from above. When it reached the quarter, the boat would lift up to meet it, allowing the breaker to rumble harmless under the boat.

They say it's hard to capture towering seas in photos. I was unable. It is an impressive thing, though, as you bob from peak to trough as happy as can be. I read that "A single four-foot wave traveling along a 100-foot front contains enough energy to power Seattle for an entire day." I could not fathom what kind of power these monsters offered. Their energy is inconceivable and a cruising boat's friendly, even soothing, interaction with them is a beautiful thing.

I have learned that one thing that requires proper installation is the SSB. It is a great source of cheap, fun, at-sea entertainment. It is frustrating when your system sucks compared to other people's, though. Mine is getting better all of the time as I get advice (and add ground plane). Still, I find myself listening to some boats that have really clear transmissions and I suffer from a mild case of signal envy.

It was at sea in the Indian Ocean that I finally achieved Sail-Mail. Before leaving Darwin, I had signed up for the SailMail SSB e-mail service ($250 a year). The only problem was I was not sure my old system would work with SailMail. With some tips and sketches from fellow cruisers I wired up some cables and finally, smailed with success. E-mailing at sea? Good fun.

Now that I was Mr. Single Side Band, I found many ways to enjoy it. In the morning, I checked in with the net. I gave them my position and heard how my friends were doing. At lunch time, I liked to tune into global news with the BBC world service. Later, I would do a little smailing and even download wind predictions (called Grib files) via SailMail. Unlike a satellite phone, I remained disconnected until I chose to reach out.

The boat CHARLOTTE, who had departed Cocos just before me, had arrived in Rodriguez. They teased me on the net with info on the nice wharf-side restaurant with three dollar meals and dollar beers. As I approached the island, I ran through

LOW KEY awaiting her mainsail off Tahaa

LOW KEY gets put back into the water, Raiatea

Onboard repairs to the entertainment system

Coldies with our friend Rick, owner Bloody Mary's,
Bora Bora

Street market, downtown Suva

Long awaited stand up shower on the beach, US Samoa

Side-tied to new friends in Sydney Harbour

Provisioning for the Yasawa Islands, Fiji

Woody, Joanie and Keith with tribal kids in Yasawas

Phil's goodbye party, Whitsunday Sailing Club

Table Mountain in majestic Cape Town, South Africa

Playing bocce with cruisers on Lizard, Great Barrier Reef

Pilot whale invasion off Brazil

Just in time for incredible Trinidad Carnival

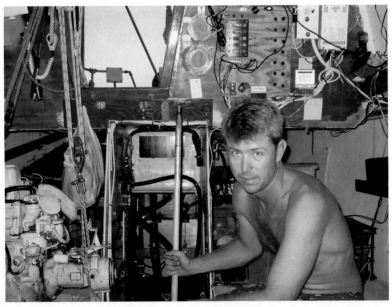

It is possible to pull your motor and drive shaft in a rolly anchorage

Fred joins me for a couple days, mid-ocean

Out with Chuck and Ann in Huatulco, Mexico

some squally weather. You know how it works: The cloud comes over, then the wind comes up and later drops off to nothing until the next cycle. You have to stay reefed for the big winds, and so you just sit in the calms. I recorded my slowest day of the trip—126 miles. Now that I think about it, that is nothing to complain about.

And finally, after 14 days, land ho! I fired up the car stereo and picked up an AM radio station. She was speaking French; it sounded nice. I jibed around the top of the island, skated just outside the big shore break, and beat up the entrance to the harbor.

CHAPTER 15

Africans!

After a bumpy 14 days from beautiful Cocos Keeling, I pulled into a little man-made anchorage etched out of a reef on an island called Rodriguez in the southern Indian Ocean. I anchored among the other cruising boats and welcomed the Health, Coast Guard and Immigration officials aboard. Turns out that the Coast Guard guy and I share the same birthdate. Eddie went on to teach me some of the local Creole language while we waited for his launch to return. Rodriguez was where French Mauritius put its slaves after they abolished slavery. A more friendly and welcoming place you would be hard pressed to find.

After check-in, I started in on the post arrival boat clean up. My fellow cruisers stopped by throughout the day to invite me for drinks/dinner etc., but I was looking forward to a nice quiet night on a cleaned-up LOW KEY with no watches. I needed good food, though, which was no longer available onboard since I took over the cooking. I snuck ashore and found an ATM on a darkened street. Neighborhoods like this at home you wouldn't go through in an armored vehicle. But my friends on the net said there was no crime here. My life clinging to a thread of hearsay, I made my way to the Restaurant Du Quai and ordered some food to go. I met Mbenga, the waiter. We talked for a few minutes. He offered me (a complete stranger) a couple of his CDs to burn for my collection. Who does that?

The next day I took the dinghy in to check out the town. As I putted up to the dock, I was waved over to tie up behind a power boat. Dirk's boat was some kinda 1970's retro sport-fish. "It's American, you know!" he exclaimed in a thick German accent while gesturing toward his boat. Some of the other cruisers had told Dirk that an American was soon arriving. I noticed that he had already hoisted a mini American flag among six others representing the nations of all his new cruising friends in the mini anchorage. A couple days later, a Japanese boat pulled in. Dirk seemed a little anxious. I don't think he had a Japanese flag.

I don't know what I was expecting from Rodriguez, but the place seemed very foreign and small and friendly and cheap and islandy. Oddly, from the people to the buildings to the lay of the land, the place was the spitting image of a stop I once made on the island of Mayreau in the Caribbean. I had been at sea alone for two weeks. The blur of colors, the activity and the human interaction were welcome.

Local flavor

The whole town seemed to be built with cinder blocks or rough cut wood, covered with corrugated roofs. Even in the good part of town, the shops were more like shacks. And I was not in the good part of town when it started to rain. It is just an old habit to duck into the nearest pub to get out of the rain. So I did and found myself standing at a bar between a couple large, rough looking African gentlemen, looking at the bartender who was either wondering what the hell I was doing there or wondering what the hell I wanted to drink. I assumed the latter and ordered a local beer. Whatever he said back to me I'll never know. I just nodded and ended up with a frosty Phoenix that cost me 20 Rupees, less than a dollar. I made my way to a dark corner and set up shop. The place was awesome. The wooden structure could have caved in at anytime under the weight of the light shower. Right across from me were some shady fellows playing cards. The shack was full of unsavory types slung low over their poison of choice. Hollywood could not have done it better. I glanced down at the chair next to me where my backpack lay and considered pulling my shiny digital camera out and snapping some shots of this hole-in-the-wall to end-all. I know, I know, I thought better of the idea.

Just as I started to relax a little and enjoy my beer (Phoenix is a great beer), one of the big guys up at the bar started yelling at me. Here we go, I thought. I scanned the place for an escape route and eased my free hand under the table and onto my bag. Escape would be easy enough since the large windows had long lost their glass. I gave him my most confident, "What's that?" In a heavy voice he repeated himself. Through his thick Creole accent I made out the words the second time. He said, "Your Phoenix, how do you like our beer?" And how nice is that, I thought? Before I left, Curtis made it very clear that I was welcome anytime in that bar. Excuse me, I think I have a tear.

On Saturday I joined a cool old Italian singlehander named Piero for a browse of the little street market. I bought tomatoes from this cute local girl but quickly found myself out-dialogued by my seasoned Italian friend (using English as a second language). It seems I still have a lot to learn about smooth talking the babes. Mauritius exports sugar cane and you know what that means: Rum! To the store we went to stock up on Mauritius' best, at $8 for a bottle.

A bunch of the cruisers arranged a dinner on Piero's big sloop. "What should I bring?" I asked. Funny how word gets around. They did not want me to bring food.

"Just bring yourself, Woody." I wanted to bring something besides my excellent boat brewed beer and humble demeanor. I brought every cruiser's favorite: ice cream. I cranked up my stand alone (Engel) fridge, procured the ice cream from shore, and was able to keep it mostly frozen until after dinner (lucky it was windy). There was another singlehander in the anchorage named Hans on a boat called BORN FREE, from Sweden.

After dinner the crowd wound down to three. Piero, Hans, and I drank a couple bottles of the local. Those guys had good stories.

The next day Piero's friends showed up in the big Italian cruiser, AMALTEA. Piero dropped by LOW KEY to inform me that AMALTEA had invited us singlehanders aboard for cocktails and, later, dinner at the restaurant. Finally, a perk to singlehanding. Mario, Izeo, Peter and Silvie took good care of us. We would be the beneficiaries of a few such evenings.

I went ashore to pick up some stuff for the boat. They had a shack/general store that seemed to have everything that China makes jammed into some nook or cranny. From there I went and found the shack with the hair cutting girls and got the best haircut I have ever had for a dollar (30 Mauritius Rupees). That seemed like a full day's work, so I moseyed over to check out this Putt Putt place I had heard so much about. It was a miniature golf place with a bar right on the beach. Funny, on my many visits, I never saw anyone putting. I found Hans, Izeo and Silvie having a couple. Hans and I found Mario later and we took him to my new favorite place. I called it "The Red Door" since none of the town's shacks had names. My friend Curtis wasn't there.

I discovered a place in town that sold blocks of cookies for 25 cents. Somehow, solo sailing was giving me a craving for sweets. Problem solved. I just had to figure out which type of cookie I liked best. I bought a block of each and, while watching a movie onboard that night, discovered that I liked them all.

Island tour?

With the guidance of a friendly local named James, a bunch of us piled into a minivan and cruised all over the island. But first things first, for any road trip you need a good stash of food. Nearby there was a roadstand where a couple cute local girls sold chicken burgers for 25 cents. I got five. I had been there before. The girls and I played this game where they would pretend to not speak English and I would speak slowly and point a lot. They would smile and nod and when I walked away, they would laugh at me. I am always happy to entertain.

The tour visited two hotels, a couple beaches, some pigs and two small public parks. There was supposed to be a stalactite cave stop, but there was some issue with permits so we skipped it. I didn't care, it was just good to be out and about in a vehicle that goes faster than 8 mph. It was fun to see the interior of an island. We see a lot of the coastal areas and forget that most of an island is out of sight of shore. Did you know that there are people that live in the middle of islands?

On the way back to the harbor, we stopped by the meteorological office. They wouldn't let us in, we were not expected, and they "can't just have people dropping in." As I looked around at all of the 1950s "weather instruments," I could see that this was a top level operation that should be taken much more seriously. A couple of the cruisers played the game and were given the tour. One of the devices consisted of a glass dome that the sun shone through. It focused down onto a piece of paper and burnt a line showing how often the sun was out that day and at what angle. Good to know that someone is keeping track of that kind of thing.

Bonus! The island used to be French and you know what that means: fresh baguettes every morning. Here's a cruising trick that works well in baguette harbors. It's more of a pyramid scheme actually. Get up early on your first day and go in and buy $1 worth of bread (ten loaves) and distribute them amongst your fellow cruisers in the bay. You won't have to worry about morning baguettes for weeks. I have said it before, cruisers are the nicest people. In my case though, I'm never in port long enough to fully capitalize on my investment.

A daily pattern developed that went something like this: Wake up to the fresh hot bread delivery, work on the boat and have lunch, head ashore for "errands," and bump into another cruiser. Visit one of the shack/bars to cool off with a quick coldie. Back to the boat to dump whatever provisions were procured in the afternoon scavenger hunt. In the evening, hook up with whomever was eating at the nice but cheap Du Quai Restaurant. And then it was back to some random boat for rums (unless you could cleverly steal away when no one was looking and head back to your own boat for popcorn and a movie).

I'm getting married!

I had to take a break from the boat work one morning to go in and meet my future ex-wife. James, our local tour guide, badly wanted me to marry a local girl. Piero and I later discussed this and decided that it was a good idea only if I could get a package deal with a marriage now and a divorce before leaving.

Piero had a big party one night on his oversized Beneteau-looking (though much heavier) Greek-designed cruiser. Part of the plan was to get the Japanese girls over so Hans and I could chat 'em up before the Canadian guys on IL GRANCHIO arrived in the bay the next day to steal them away. Things were going well (far as I know) until I turned around and they were gone. They had been ushered out quietly by the parents, without so much as a goodbye. Don't look at me like that, they were in their twenties! The party went late. Classic scene of the evening? Dirk, getting a ride back to his boat in Hans' dinghy, hunkered down behind the rail, mowing down imaginary foes with his imitation machine gun. Hans wasn't amused (still cracks me up!).

The day before I left, Thomas, from the steel ketch CHAR-LOTTE, swung by LOW KEY with his old Aries windvane parts. He had rebuilt his windvane and insisted that mine could use a tune up. He was right. We found that one of the main plastic parts was cracked and about to give out. Also, the rudder breakaway tube had a vertical stress crack in it (maybe it's not designed to surf at 15 knots). I started to think about single-handed life at sea with no wind vane steering. The thought gave me chills—the bad ones. Thanks Thomas!

It was early on departure day and I could not sleep. There was still much to do in preparation for the big sail ahead. I made a cover for the companionway hatch out of old sail cloth and I pumped silicone into all of the seams of my dodger. I had previously done this to the forward facing zippers and it worked well. My dodger is real pretty, it just doesn't keep the water out when waves are spilling over the boat. I have two words for you: hard dodger! You will probably never see a cruising boat with its soft dodger folded down. That is the only advantage I can think of for the canvas dodger. A hard dodger can be built in any shape you like for less money. You can attach stuff to it, like solar panels and hand rails, you don't have to replace it every few years, and most important to me, it is less likely to leak.

Making license plates

I went to town for the last time. I stopped by the bakery first. I got three fat pastries and five oversized baguettes. "Thirty lira, you say? Oh, O.K." All of that for a dollar. I stopped by Customs to check out. It quickly became apparent that I had never checked in. Of all the people that came aboard my boat that first day, none of them were Customs. And this is my problem? The mood turned sour in a hurry. "You have committed an offense!" he exclaimed and he left the room. I gathered my stuff together because you know how things can get misplaced when someone gets arrested. I have been arrested before, a couple of times in California and once in Texas, and I was kind of looking forward to seeing the facilities. But unfortunately (for the story's sake), it was not to be. He came back smiling. Someone higher up (the great grand master of Rodriguez officialdom) had been consulted and my by-the-letter Indian friend was instructed to just fill out the paperwork now and date it for my arrival day. I could have told him that.

I had a master plan to buy food and spend every last cent, except for a couple of coins for my mini treasure chest. I hit the biggest "store" and bought some groceries, expecting to have a bunch of lira left over to go back in and buy them out of the nearly free cookies. My bill came out exactly to the money I had. I could not get one batch of cookies! All that research for naught. It was going to be a long trip.

I got back to the boat and enjoyed one last meal before heading back to sea. On my way out of the anchorage, cruisers on the other boats came out on deck to wave goodbye and sound their horns. I had never had that happen before. I have had boats throw vegetables . . . just kidding. It was nice. Was it the longer, harder legs that we are all having to do that had brought us closer together? Or was it because I was the first boat to try for the coast of Africa "too early" in the season and they thought I'd never make it? I like the first reason.

I maneuvered LOW KEY out of the marked channel and shut the engine down. I drifted downwind in 20 knots while rigging the boat. For long trips I take the anchor off the bow and lash it to the rail amidships. I tie the dinghy upside down over the windlass.

I looked over my shoulder in the fading twilight and saw the lights of the channel markers by town. I searched and couldn't find the range lights that would lead me safely through the outer reef. Maybe the range wasn't lit. I looked toward the sea and noticed that the outer reef buoys definitely weren't lit. I had a couple miles to go and was only doing two knots without sails. I had charted a route through the gap on the GPS. Not being the most patient sailor, I pulled up the #2 headsail and ripped on out on my plotted line. I never saw the two buoys. And finally, I was back at sea!

It was a beautiful stop, and I met some quality people and made some new friends. Still, it was great to be back out there, finally starting on the dreaded leg to South Africa. Of the three

2,000nm legs from Darwin to Durban, it was this last leg that would take me around the bottom of Madagascar and through the Agulhas current where 20-meter, boat-sinking, breaking seas are a common occurrence. As Bitchin would say, "If cruising were easy, everybody would be doing it." The sun set, the boat was happy; I drifted off to sleep.

CHAPTER 16

The Last Leg

After a little break on the small Mauritian island of Rodriguez, I was back at sea to start the last of three sailing legs from Australia to South Africa. I would start out sailing LOW KEY SW to get below the shelf of Madagascar and then WSW to finally close with the coast of South Africa. Right at the end we would have to cross the dreaded Agulhas Current. Cyclones barreling down from the north, southerlies busting up from the south, this was offshore sailing at its craziest.

Sixty miles out from Rodriguez I passed the point on the globe that was as far away as I would get from where we started in California. I thought about how far I had come and the challenges yet to be faced. Beating up the coast of Mexico may prove to be the most difficult sailing, but the water just ahead held the most potential for disaster. The cruising guides talked about the 65-foot breaking seas brought on by 50-knot southerlies pushing against a six-knot current. The waves push up and fall on boats literally crushing them. The southerlies sweep through four out of seven days this time of year. My cruising friends in Rodriguez had warned that I was departing too early. I was banking on the seasonal shift to come early this year. The Indian Ocean had already had a very early cyclone develop in its north and the water was getting warm already.

The leg started out with light wind. I had not seen light conditions for over a month. I took the opportunity to finish up the project list aimed at preparing LOW KEY for knockdown conditions. First things first, I installed the lee cloths for more comfortable sleeping in big seas. I had put out the jack lines for safer working on deck. I installed eyes in the cockpit for securing the gear there, eyes for the hatch boards to keep them onboard, sliding catches to keep the heavier tools in their lockers, and a system of slide bolts and line to secure the oven. Ovens are known to pop out of their gimbals during a knockdown, roll around the cabin and take out a port or window. I checked that the emergency tiller worked and rigged a float free system for the dinghy so I would only be responsible for coming up with the ditch kit in the event of a quick roll and sink. Though the hull is solid glass, I am not sure she would come back up if dumped onto her light weight cabin top. Basically, I did a lot of projects I could have done before leaving my slip back home.

I find sailing alone fun . . . now. It took some getting used to. I admit that when I left Australia I was not an instant fan of singlehanding. They say that you have to be comfortable with yourself, and that had me worried. Now that I had been sailing alone for two months, I had decided that I liked me. Also, you are not responsible for anyone else when sailing solo. There is comfort in that. But mostly, the satisfaction comes in accomplishing things all on your own. Still, like most beautiful experiences, I suspect it would be even better shared. And yes, I talk to myself. Hell, you can sing aloud when there's no one around. Question: If you are singing 1,000 miles from land and no one is there to hear it, does it still sound bad?

Around the bottom of Madagascar, I started seeing a lot of traffic. I must have been on the center divider of shipping lanes because I had ships passing me on both sides in opposite directions. I started calling the ships on 16. There were a lot of cruisers behind me and I wanted the ships that traverse the area to be aware that there were people in small boats out here. Usually I would just say hello and ask where they were going and wish them a nice trip. If I needed it, I would ask for a weather update. Sometimes I would ask if my boat shows up on their radar. It never does. Even with my reflector in the rigging, their radars are tuned up so high that they can only see other large ships. Keep in mind that only you are looking out for you.

I was reading *The Ocean Almanac* that Tania had given me about great voyages, Vikings, pirates, sea creatures and a bunch of other nautical-type subjects. There was a section on living sea monsters and, specifically, giant squid that were found in the very same waters that I was sailing. Giant squid measuring 50 feet were known to "attack" boats that had surprised them by grappling their hulls with their endless tentacles. So it was no surprise when I awoke one morning and found four of them doing just that! Granted, they were not the fully grown ones. On deck, mine were only a few inches long, but had I come upon them 20 or 30 years from now, I would surely be in trouble!

The wind had picked up and we were sailing along splendidly, on course for Durban. Ever present was a very large SW swell, a reminder of the big weather constantly brewing in the roaring forties to the south.

Lost to the sea

I had made two notable mistakes since I left California. My first was when I accidentally cut a hard-to-replace electronic cable. My second was not bringing the dinghy aboard while riding out a mini storm at anchor which resulted in a lost oar. I now had a third, much larger, error to haunt me. For 18 months I had stowed the headsails in their bags on deck without incident. Just two weeks before, I had started tying them down in preparation for the more serious conditions of the devil's coast. Old habits die hard, and I left "the whomper" unlashed on a particularly rolly night. The sail slipped over the side unnoticed. I was disappointed with myself. I had lost one of my most loyal crew. The big sail was always there for me and I had let it down. Still, I had an ocean to finish crossing, so I didn't think on it much then.

After a nap one afternoon, I awoke and stepped out into the cockpit. The boat was happily doing her thing, blazing down course, just the sound of the water rushing by. It was beautifully sunny and warm, and the ocean was that inky blue that you get, well, everywhere when offshore. It occurred to me that I could have been anywhere on any ocean. Night time was different. At night the stars lit up a mystery. The night sky here was very different from the one I was raised with.

I started tuning into the weather nets on the SSB. Land based stations would tell you your area forecast based on the South African Weather Service forecasts. But it was like they were predicting the weather from the moon. I learned not to take the forecasts too seriously. On the cruising net someone checked in from Zanzibar. There is an island called Zanzibar! I know I am moving too fast if I am missing places like the island of Zanzibar. I'll just have to figure a way to go around again and catch some of the great stuff I missed.

And finally, I was approaching the coast. The heaviest part of the Agulhas Current runs just 20 miles offshore. My SailMail grib files were predicting I would have light wind. South African weather contradicted that report with, ". . . big south winds coming." It was the south winds slamming into the huge current that caused all the sinkings along the coast. What to do? I would have been in Durban already if I hadn't taken previous South African Weather Service advice and slowed down. I sped back up but it was too late. I sailed right into a dead calm in the thick of the current.

Land Ho!

That night I saw the high burn glow of Durban, my ocean crossing objective. It was just over the horizon. The glow was moving to the north. I was being swept south at a quick pace. Forget that, I fired up the motor. I was too excited to finally make landfall to wait for wind and sail in. I turned on the radio and tuned into South African music and to people speaking strange languages. LOW KEY and I motored all night, listening to the sounds of Africa, and with the first rays of sunrise, we made the turn that put us behind the breakwall at Durban. After sailing over 6,000 miles, I had crossed the Indian Ocean. And I had done it by myself. I hadn't given it much thought until then. I was feeling pretty great.

I found the marina right downtown in an area with big city-like buildings. I was headed to the vagrant, I mean, visitors dock when I spotted Craig. I met Craig, a South African guy, in Rodriguez. He was there with his friends to deliver the boat CARE FREE back to its home in Durban. He motioned me into a slip on the real docks. Craig took my lines and walked me to his club, the Royal Natal Yacht Club. As we walked, I asked about Customs and all the check-in stuff. He waved the suggestion off. It was first things first in Durban.

At the club I met the manager Steve and had a beer and a shower, and only then was I released to meet with Customs. The Customs guy came down to the boat, and Immigration met me at the top of the docks. The check in was easy. By this time, Bob, who represented the competing yacht club, had found the new visitor and dragged me to PYC. We had another coldy. I stopped by and said hello to my friends on the big cruiser AMALTEA. We all ended up over at the Royal Natal for the Braai (BBQ). Later that night, I met my new friends, Priya and Raakhi, a couple of local Indian girls who took me in and showed me the sights during my stay in Durban.

A couple of things about Durban. The marina area is great. You have most everything you need within a block of your boat. But as you try to venture further, you encounter some friction from the locals. The truth is they are concerned for your safety. I was continuously told to be careful by both people around the dock and by people in town. Apparently, there are roving gangs of knife-wielding teenagers who are after your cash and valuables. Doing my best low-end backpacker impersonation, I went to town a lot and didn't have any problems.

The next afternoon, Priya came down and picked me up to take me to the movies. They had a shop in the mall that sold beef jerky! It's called biltong in South Africa and it was excellent. That night, Raakhi took me out to dinner with her three friends. Just the four girls and I. How nice was that? Pretty nice. On another night, they took me to this shark encounter place and then to dinner and dancing and back to this big house in the hills one of them lived in. We had a great time.

I met Tony at his shop, Cruising Connections, by the marina. Being a cruiser himself, Tony looks after his own. He gave me three charts and a cruising guide in trade for my big East African Pilot book. Tony would see me often because I would continually come by his shop and bug him about all kinds of things from local weather to where to get things fixed. Next door to Tony was Seaport Marine Supply. Salish and Nick and the gang run the best chandlery I had seen in a while. If they didn't have it, they got it for you that afternoon.

The yacht OCEAN PHOENIX arrived and parked by AMALTEA on the visitors' dock. It was crowded over there. I had met the crew, Charlie and Gabrielle, in Rodriguez. With the group from AMALTEA, we all met up for dinner at the Royal Natal that evening. It was a really fun crowd. Later that week, John and Maggie would invite me, DOS TINTOS, and the four Canadian kids on IL GRANCHIO (20 year olds) over to OCEAN PHOENIX for cocktails and great grub. Another great evening with good people.

The cruising situation around South Africa looks like this. You can only sail south on the odd north wind because the predominant southerlies cause the massive waves. The first safe harbor south of Durban is 255 miles away. Waiting for a two-day north wind could trap you in Durban for weeks. I know. I was there for two long ones. But there were many factors conspiring to keep me in Durban. The SA weather forecasting was one of them. The forecasts would shift around dramatically in a six-hour period and still end up not being accurate. But the weather obstacle proved to be a non-issue once I began my port clearance odyssey. Durban is home to the most unbelievably, almost comically, complex check-out procedure I had yet endured. The port makes a potentially dangerous sailing situation worse by making it so very difficult to leave when you finally get your weather window.

And the last obstacle to leaving was the people I met in Durban. Durban may well go down as the most friendly stop of my adventure (with Sydney and Airlie in the mix). They wouldn't let me leave. There was always some fun event coming up and, "you should stay because the next weather window looks even better." I want to say thanks to all the guys and gals which made my Durban visit such a warm one!

The bottom of the world

But escape I did. As great as Durban was, it was good to be back at sea. The sail started out slow. The wind was light. Distant squall lines and the lure of the big southbound current tempted me further offshore. Find the current I did . . . and the wind. With 20 knots of wind just aft of the beam and four knots of current, LOW KEY was doing over 10 knots. That much current makes for a bumpy ride, bumpy but fast. We did 212 nm in 24 hours. That's a big number for a little boat. I blew right by the first port, East London, and sailed on for Port Elizabeth. Off Port Elizabeth I used my cell phone to call Tony back in Durban, and he checked the weather for me and gave me the thumbs up to keep going. Sweet. I tacked back out and found my current again.

Following the coast, I was finally able to start turning in a west direction. I was aiming for Knysna. Sheldon and Michele who worked on boats back in Durban said the port was not to be missed. Besides having a very impressive towering entrance, Knysna also had Michele's sister who was available to show me the sights. It sounded like a good place to stop. But I had good wind. I know, I need to seriously consider a change in priorities. Looking back, it was a bad call. I needed to arrive at the top of the flood tide during the day to negotiate the entrance. That meant that I had to sit off the port for 14 hours. As it was, I sailed by and then lost the wind. I sat 60 miles offshore and only made 100 miles in three days. I could have been hanging out in Knysna for those days.

Still, it was fun sitting off the bottom of Africa. One night I parked by a big oil rig. It was dead calm, glassy water. I shut down the engine just before sunset with the rig about a half mile away. As soon as I came to a stop, the sea lions showed up. Very curious, they all just had to have a look. One at a time they would pop their heads up from the water about 20 feet away. After a great sunset, I noticed that the rig had a giant flame coming from one of the spars. It was like having my own fireplace. To the sounds of sea lions breathing, I drifted off to sleep.

The night before rounding Cape Agulhas, the wind came back up. The night was moonless and so the stars were super bright. And then I saw them. INCOMING TORPEDOES!! Oh, they're just dolphins. When the dolphins come and play at night, you can't see them except for their outline and a long trail drawn in the glowing phosphorescence. Very cool. My dolphin friends hung out for over an hour. With my feet over the bow I could almost touch them.

It was a beautiful day when I rounded the Cape, sunny and warm. At 34 degrees south, the Cape is the same latitude as Los Angeles (in the northern hemisphere). It was a good feeling to make the turn to the north and to start heading back toward palm trees and coconuts where I belong.

I kept all the sails up as the wind built. If something was going to break, I wanted it to break then instead of on my next big leg. It was a fast run into Cape Town. I arrived at night after a week at sea. The guys in Durban would later tell me that only a couple boats had ever made the whole trip on one weather window. I had a guest coming and I had to prep the boat for her and our upcoming South Atlantic crossing. At over 3,500 nautical miles, the South Atlantic crossing would be my longest sail ever. I was hoping to arrive in time for Christmas—Christmas in Brazil.

CHAPTER 17

Cape Town, South Africa

*"This Cape is the most stately thing and the fairest
Cape we saw in the entire circumference of the earth."*
—SIR FRANCIS DRAKE

I approached Cape Town at night. It's true, even now it is an unbelievable sight, massive Table Mountain rising up from the middle of the glow of the city. The air had a West African chill. It was a crystal clear night as I sailed full speed into the lee of the mountain. It was 0300 but I wasn't tired. Cape Town would mark the end of hard sailing for LOW KEY for a while. It was a welcome landfall.

I parked at the Royal Cape Yacht Club and checked in. It had started to rain. Back at the boat I fired up the lantern and spent the rest of the day cozily finishing up e-mail, listening to the rain fall on the cabin roof, and resting. It was race day at the Royal Cape and they took their racing seriously. I watched the boats prep and go while I savored a frosty draft at the club.

First things first, in order to enter Brazil I needed to get a visa. Bright and early the next morning, I checked in with Cape Town Customs before finding the Brazilian consulate downtown. It was Friday and I had intended to leave Tuesday morning. The Brazilian girl at the desk suggested that the process could not be completed by then. I looked her in the eye to encourage some enthusiasm, using the Jedi mind trick. We agreed that it was possible and that we would both try. I left with a large list of tasks to be accomplished by 3:00 pm. Cool, a challenge.

Across the street was a passport photo place—done. They also had Internet access. I ripped off a quick e-mail to my friend Anthony, who was looking after my mail, asking him to fax a copy of my current documentation to the consulate. I wanted to call him to confirm. My phone list was back on the boat, so I searched online and found Ant's home phone number. Not home. I e-mailed a friend of a guy that Ant worked with to tell him that I urgently needed Ant to check his e-mail or phone messages. Ant was on vacation, but John knew where to find him. I printed, again from the Internet, copies of my credit card statements with large credit lines and 0 balances. The consulate probably would have preferred to see a checking account, but I was sure mine would not impress them. I arrived back at the consulate that afternoon to find that Ant had indeed been found and had once again come through for me. After admitting to and explaining convictions I had for minor offences back home, we were back on schedule. Being from a different culture, she had trouble believing that one could get arrested for urinating on a tree.

My crew for the South Atlantic crossing arrived and met me at the boat. Donna was an engineer, a commercial pilot and a PADI rescue diver. Donna would later describe *Latitudes & Attitudes* as ". . . not my kind of publication." Excuse me? She had had some offshore experience. When people contact me to join a leg on LOW KEY, they enter into a strict screening process. Basically, I don't care if you've ever sailed. If I think we can get along for the duration of the trip (you don't sound psychotic), then I say, "Come on down." For open ocean legs away from land (where I can't put you ashore) I also want to know if you are prone to getting seasick. And this is for your comfort only. But that's about all I'm interested in. Experience. What you don't know, I will teach you. It's easier to teach you the ins and outs of sailing/cruising if you do not already have bad habits. Donna joined me in town for some errands. After which we found the only pub on the planet that does not sell French fries.

Donna's entry: *"1:30 pm by my Swiss Army watch, and I'm still in the Customs office at Cape Town's International Airport trying to make my way to the Royal Yacht Club and a grand adventure. The agents don't want to grant entry as I do not have a return plane ticket—I try to explain that I'm not leaving by plane, but by sailboat to Recife, Brazil. How do I know the owner of the boat? Well, I don't. He's on his way around the world and I'm joining him on this leg of the trip. They're not convinced; who sails 3,600 nautical miles across the South Atlantic in a 33-foot sailboat with someone they've never met? I did.*

My guess is that most people are presented with extraordinary opportunities throughout their lives, but reject those opportunities without first giving them full notice. This adventure started with a trip to Barnes and Noble one evening—Tania Aebi's book was displayed on the shelves marked "Staff Recommends." I picked up a copy and headed for a latte in the back of the store. Three months later, I'd purchased and restored my 19-foot Starwind cruiser, POLARIS, and was already thinking about bigger boats, deserted islands and life at sea.

Cincinnati isn't exactly a sailing Mecca and so we live vicariously through the photos in the various sailing magazines and surf the Internet for good deals. It occurred to me that, other than overall lust, I had no idea what to look for in a boat. I tend go for the good looking "bad boy." Not such an issue on our Ohio lakes, but probably not the right approach to finding a home suitable of weathering the high seas. And so, flipping through the classifieds in Latitudes & Attitudes *one evening, I found an ad that invited me to "sail with*

Captain Woody." I laughed to myself and fired off an e-mail. An opportunity.

To my surprise, Woody wrote back—he was in Darwin on his way to Cocos, Rodriguez and then Durban and suggested either the leg from Durban to Cape Town, or the leg from Cape Town to Recife, Brazil. The latter would take about a month, but should be good sailing and an opportunity to learn something about boats. We wrote back and forth over the next couple of months, and in September I bought a ticket to Cape Town.

At the airport, the Customs agents finally decided that it was just too hot and that my midwest mannerly in-your-face directness wasn't worth an argument about return tickets, and let me go. A left turn out of the yacht club office to the end of the pier, turn right then left again and another right—there she was: dark blue with tan colored sail covers, lines, buckets and fresh water containers, and all the sundries you'd expect from a boat sailed halfway around the world—LOW KEY, Woody's 33-foot Cal. Woody's laid-back southern California smile greeted me and I knew I'd made the right decision—it was going to be a great trip."

Tourists

Donna, a cruiser named Chris, and I took the topless bus tour of the city. A glaring example of false advertising, I would discover, because the only thing that would be topless on the tour was the bus. Still, it was a beautiful day in Cape Town which was too small to know smog. What sets it apart from any other city I've seen is the amazing backdrop of Table Mountain and its towering neighbors. The tour guide talked sympathetically about their struggle with apartheid but lost me with his play by play of the particulars of this historic building and that one. He did get my attention for a sec when he mentioned with a gleam in his eye that his beloved Cape Town aspired to be like New

York City some day. This drew the comment from Donna, "Clearly he's never been there." Cape Town had its own appeal.

The bus took us part way up Table Mountain. After a much deserved ice cream, Donna, Chris and I took the cable car to the top. The views were awesome. The clouds ran up the windward side and careened over the top of our heads, shredding themselves on the jagged edges. We decided to skip the tram ride down and hike the trail that led back to the topless buses. It was a beautiful hike down with Cape Town below us. The trail was real steep though, and the haul was long enough that I was a little sore the next day. My co-hikers would later suffer from partial incapacitation. The bus wound us down to a perfect little beach town on the other side of the mountain. The hot sand and babes and great weather made me think of home and, for a sec, miss it just a little. Donna took us out to lunch. Quality people, fun place, good food—"wonder what the rich people are doing" type of afternoon.

The bus finally dropped us at the touristy part of town. It is a big wharf/shopping/marina/pub area on the bay. There we bumped into Captain Charlie and my favorite Swiss/German, sweet Gabrielle—both from the yacht OCEAN PHOENIX. We had a couple of coldies and decided to meet up later at a restaurant we had heard about on the tour.

Mesopotamia was very cool. The five of us sat on giant pillows around a low wooden table. The walls and ceiling were adorned with Persian rugs and decor. Our waiter brought us a four-foot diameter tray of food dishes to choose from. We said yes. Again with the good people, food, wine, etc . . . and then— out came the dancer. She undulated, twisted and grooved her way through the room and into our hearts, pulling willing dance partners from the transfixed diners. We hit a jazz place next and soon lost Donna and Chris to a cab. Charlie, Gabby and I crossed the street and entered a seedy local joint where bodies were packed tight and grooving to the underground sounds.

Monday came around and I picked up my visa with a smile. We started up the get-outa-Dodge shuffle: Portnet, Immigration, Customs, shopping, Internet, boat visiting and the filling of water and fuel before a last meal at the club.

The treacherous South Atlantic

And finally, we departed Cape Town for the 3,500-mile sail to Brazil. What did I expect? They (you know, the people who seem to know everything about everything) told me to expect easy light conditions the whole trip. Well, I don't know where *they* had been sailing, but the oceans that I had crossed lately had all had some bumpy spots. *They* also said that we would be beating for the first few days. In this case, they were right. Out of the gate we charged into it. Under full sail we beat into a light headwind and mini-swell for the first few days. I thought it was beautiful. I never get to beat, and this version of beating was especially kind. My fair crew was not so enthusiastic.

At first I thought Donna was just tired. Some of us exhaust ourselves on land and take advantage of our precious time at sea to rest. I learned that this wasn't the case for her. Donna was being quietly seasick. Eventually we took her off watch duty and I slipped into singlehanding mode. I would sleep when I felt like it and look around as I could. I had the radar detector for the big ships, but the little ones could still sneak up to us. I tacked past a large oil rig and headed offshore into the vast Atlantic.

Three days in is the breaking point for most people who are seasick. Your body, having waited long enough for you to fix the problem, takes matters into its own hands and severs the communication between your inner ear and your brain, allowing your nausea to dissipate . . . or it doesn't. Donna didn't seem to be getting better. The coast of Namibia was a hundred miles to starboard and starting to veer away. I had to give Donna her options—get better or warm up her Swahili. And then, suddenly, the next morning she was better.

Donna: *"Two days and several coolies later, we set sail leaving Table Rock to our backs and the wind in our face. The weather was nice; warm and sunny, but as I mentioned, Cincinnati isn't exactly a sailing Mecca and shortly, I introduced myself to the rail. The rail and I became fast friends for several days. Off the coast of Namibia, Woody started talking about heading for shore or detouring to St. Helena—I was pretty sick and embarrassed. We'd established a three-hour watch schedule; I'd not been able to keep my last two and in addition to the seasickness, was homesick. All the questions you'd imagine came like waves—what was I thinking? I'd just missed Thanksgiving with my family and would probably miss Christmas too and on top of it all, wasn't even a help to my sailing partner. That next morning I came up on deck and faced the stern, looking back toward Cape Town. That would be quitting—and I don't quit anything. Woody said that overcoming seasickness was in your head. Just decide not to be sick. He was right."*

We sailed north at first to stay in the favorable wind and current. Cape Town was chilly, so it was good to know that we were sailing toward warmer waters. The winds for most of the trip were light, which kept the swell down. We had to pay attention to the windpilot, though, or it would stray. Also, we ran the engine from time to time to keep the batteries up. There wasn't even enough wind for the wind generator. When the motor was on we would usually make some water.

Our days took on a routine, which tends to develop on longer passages. We did our watches, fished, read and wrote, practiced our knots or watched the dolphins play at the bow. In the evening we would play music, have some home brew and good food, and watch the sun go down together.

On the bigger boats we often would have a competition between the watch crews, betting on sightings and arrival times to specific milestones. We did the same for this trip. Each day we would estimate the miles that the boat would cover by the next day–1 point. Spotting dolphins–1 point. Seeing whales or turtles or a ship on another's watch–2 points. Guessing the crossing day and time of each of the 3, 2, and 1 thousand miles-to-go points–2 points. Claiming the "Land Ho" prize–5 points. Guessing the day and time of our arrival–10 points.

Donna: *"Three hours of sleep at sea was like a full eight hours in my own bed. At home I have a feather top for my queen sized bed; on the boat I had a bunk with a cozy pillow and a lee cloth to keep me in place. The first couple of weeks out of Cape Town found the nights cool and us on watch in our foulies. At home I have a place for everything and everything in its place; on the boat, I found that I didn't need much that I couldn't put under my pillow and have close at hand—my sweatshirt, shorts, sweatpants and sox as I moved from one day climate to another at night. My foulies found a home under the companionway steps. After my late evening watch, I'd curl up in my bunk not able to get warm. I'd wake to find that he'd tucked the Army blanket around my feet as I slept, or given me an extra hour from his watch. These things he balanced with reminders about boat safety—the importance of tying knots correctly and looking after my long girlhair so as not to clog the bilge. Until now, such things had not held much weight—my girlknots sufficed for lake sailing. Scrambling about on deck at night in stiff winds trying to wrestle a 30-lb. whisker pole to the other side of the deck, groping for lines tied off to raise or lower sails, and the importance of jibing without shredding the sails all had new meaning. Out here, I could hurt someone."*

Man Overboard!

(Person Overboard?) I was down below, writing on the laptop, when I heard a slightly panicked call for help. I came up on deck to find Donna clinging for dear life on the wrong side of the lifelines. I helped her back onboard. To her credit, she never actually got wet. The jokes about Donna getting her sea legs "soon enough" would carry us right up to the coast of Brazil.

Twelve days into our sail we crossed the Prime Meridian. Sailing in light air and flat seas, we watched the GPS tick over from east longitude to west. It was a milestone of sorts for me. I was back in my own half of the world.

Swimming with us we discovered a pair of dorado (that's how slow we were going). They were swooping out from under the boat to feed on the baby flying fish. I decided to do some feeding of my own, so I rigged some fishing line to one of the arrows from my bow and tried my hand at bow-fishing. As one would come up to the surface to feed, I would let fly the arrow. Let me just say that the process was a long way from being perfect. In other words, we had pasta that night. Still, dorado next to the boat just won't do with two hungry carnivores aboard, two weeks from their next fresh meat, with a BBQ bolted to the stern rail. We dropped a line in the water and hooked up right away. That little fish provided two BBQed fillets to go with our pizza that night. I felt kinda bad since there were two dorado and they were likely mates—so we had fillets the next night, too.

Donna: "*The moon and stars rose clearly around 2100, so by the time I took my early watch at 0200, constellations had taken shape overhead; constellations that actually looked like the pictures in my field guide, but with such brilliance they cast shadows on the sea. My first morning on watch, a large grouping rose over the horizon—one very bright star with a band below, and below, one that shone like a small moon. The Southern Cross—we were in the southern hemisphere—that must be it! I was elated—Stephen Stills and Jimmy Buffett both singing in my head, I couldn't wait for Woody to wake up to share the moment. 0200 I called down, "Woody—it's time." As he came up the companionway steps in his foulies, I pointed. "Look! The Southern Cross!! Isn't it beautiful?"*

Quietly he turned and smiled. "That's Orion. The Southern Cross is over here," he added, pointing to a faint kite-like constellation across the port stern."

Sixteen days out, we passed our half-way point. Donna got the points. D12-W4 was the tally at the top of that day's log. I started to notice a trend. She was also winning most of the dailies and, because we were moving so slow, was set to win the arrival 10 points. I would have to pick up my game—or was it too late? I kept busy during that part of the trip with projects such as brewing, maintenance, and smailing through a SailMail station in Chile from mid-ocean! I even tuned the SSB into the South African weather for old times sake. I got a report that the wind would drop altogether where we were. This was good news. I had learned to interpret their offshore forecasts as consistently being the opposite. Sure enough, the wind picked up the next day.

Also keeping us busy was the twice-daily jibe. LOW KEY will sail nicely DDW (dead down wind), but with a 30-degree wind shift, always across the stern, we were challenged to hold course. I wasn't used to having someone else help me with the sails. It took some getting used to.

Late one night I awoke to an excited Donna in the companionway trying to show me something. It seemed that a flying fish had flown into her and that she had caught it. Donna had never even seen a flying fish before and here she was holding a live one, extending the fish wings for me . . . over my bunk. In my travels I have wrestled a shark and been attacked by a dugong, neither of which inspired fear in me. But get that slimy smelly thing near my bunk and panic sets in. I made her put it back.

Donna: *"I made bread once a week. Woody made noodles for lunch and ensured homebrew for the duration. The first week I worried while he was on deck as I slept.*

A foolish worry as he's sailed three-fourth of the distance around the world without my help, but a worry none the less. By the second half of the trip I settled into calmness and stopped counting days. Tuesday became Saturday and the nearness of Brazil not something I wanted to consider. I wanted a deserted island. With fresh water and coconuts. Warm breezes and palm trees. Fish. I borrowed his sarong one warm evening and vowed to burn my business suits and convince the bank I work for to institute Fridays as ultra business casual."

About 1,000 miles out, the wind finally came up and stayed. We had the big headsail up, poled out. LOW KEY took off. "Should we reef? Should we reef?" Donna asked. I had been reefing "early and often" at the beginning of the leg, trying to conserve the sails. But we were close now and the boat was stable, surfing but stable. It took a day for the new swell to find its rhythm, but it eventually did and things got flat and fast—freight train mode. As the swell would sneak up from behind, LOW KEY would put her bow down and run off surfing every chance she got. Inside the boat, one could also appreciate the sudden rush of speed by way of the rumbling sound that permeated the hull.

The points competition continued and I was doing much better. After getting 2 points for spotting a ship on Donna's watch, I had pulled within 1. D16-W15. And, of course, there were more boat projects to keep us busy. We fitted the emergency tiller as the laminated one was disintegrating and was making a racket. The new one, a sealed wheel barrel handle, was a perfect fit. Peace and quiet. I found out why my SSB tuner wasn't tuning—a couple wires plugged into the wrong slots.

Christmas Eve

And then at last, "Land Ho"—Brazil off the port bow—five points for Woody (though the points came a little too late). Log entry: "After 30 days of towering seas, violent storms, and near starvation, we have sighted land. Only by the glory of God." But the fact is that I have never sailed such a large body of water that was so entirely dormant. It was a slow but beautiful crossing, as much as anyone could hope for. The ocean had lived up to its tame reputation.

CHAPTER 18

Land Ho!

It took 30 days to sail the 3,500 miles from Cape Town, South Africa to Recife, Brazil. That's 30 days out of sight of land. I have done a few ocean crossings but this one was the longest in both distance and duration. It was long but it was mellow. I wasn't complaining. Slow means easy on equipment and except for missing a bucket, LOW KEY had arrived much the same as she had left. We pulled behind the reef and sailed by the big ships parked along the waterfront. Donna got some cat calls from the longshoremen. Good to see that some things are the same wherever you go.

We made our way to the back of the bay through the sticks that indicated the deep water. The channel lead us to Club Iate Cabanga. With the help of a marina worker who only spoke Portuguese and French, we Med-moored next to a big ex-cruiser. The boat had become a permanent fixture, tied to the sea wall. Someone's dream had come to an end in this little marina in Brazil. We had our showers, and they were beautiful, before heading over to the office. No one spoke English there either. No worries, I had been practicing my Portuguese on the sail over. Actually, that turned out to be a waste of time. Through hand signals and written Spanish we sorted out that Immigration was closed and that the only place open to eat was the mall and that a taxi could take us there. Cool!

It was Christmas Eve. Donna was happy to eat something on the boat, but I was fired up to have something fresh. We cabbed to the old town, to the new mall and got a big salad and a glass of wine. We went back to the boat, set up the TV in the saloon and partook of some home brew and watched a couple of movies to celebrate our arrival/Christmas Eve.

The next day the yacht club restaurant was open and so we sat down to a big brunch with a bunch of overflowing cheeseburgers and fries. Poolside were the high-end Brazilian families enjoying a Christmas afternoon at the club. We took Donna to the airport to check on flights for her. High consumption-ville: air-conditioning, elevators, fast food and airplanes. We sat and watched some of them land. Donna, being a pilot, made the viewing much more interesting.

We had a cab drop us at the Praia (the beach) where we were immediately offered chairs and more coldies. Were they expecting me? We drank from large frosty bottles while watching volleyball and locals all afternoon. Our tab was $8. Donna took us out for a big Christmas yacht club dinner. Recife was a place where you could get filet mignon at a nice restaurant for under $10.

The next day I found the big screen and couch combo in the TV room that no one else seemed to know about. I flipped around and found a news station from the States. After listening to the BBC for three months I was ready for the watered down U.S. version of the news. All over the tube were pictures and stories of vast devastation in Sri Lanka, Indonesia and Thailand. Tens of thousands were dead or missing. It was the coverage of the big tsunami. It was hard to see that kind of thing. Thailand was where my friends Dave and Flippa were! I was supposed to be there with them and my friends on MAN-DARA. Part of me wished I was, if just to help out. But then I tend to park near the beach in 10 feet of water. It could have been bad news for LOW KEY and me in the shallows. I would get an e-mail from Dave the next day. He said he was O.K. and told his story. I forwarded it to *Latitudes & Attitudes* for publication.

Checking in

To start our check-in procedure, I went by the office for any advice they might have. One of the guys there that day spoke some English. He told me where to go to start the process and mentioned that I should wear long pants and shoes. I already had my nicest shorts on (and it was really really hot in Brazil). As I left the office to head back to the boat, I saw a beautiful painting on the wall. It was a depiction of the first meeting of the bright-eyed, blissful, half-naked locals and the evil missionaries. They were probably telling them to put some more clothes on. I like the island cultures that decided that they would be better off if they ate the missionaries. They always seem so much happier. Who needs a church when love and community are the cornerstones of your culture?

My check-in/out procedure was a long-drawn-out process that lasted three days. Whatever the sea had thrown at us on this voyage, this was worse. One of the highlights was being sent to the airport (one of three times) to be fingerprinted and photographed. The U.S. was doing it to them and so we get the same treatment abroad. I also had to get a yellow fever shot. The electricity at the medical center was out so they couldn't open the inoculation fridge because it would let the cold out . . . and on and on. My personal Groundhog Day continued. Halfway through the process, Donna flew out. For a sec, I envied her.

But like with any boat project, throw enough hours at it and it gets done. And it did get done and I was cleared to leave port. Back at the yacht club, I had a couple of coldies sent over to the TV room to celebrate a job finally done. I later paid my slip fee ($20 for four days) and prepped the boat to leave. I wanted to leave on an outgoing tide so I slept some and then departed Recife just before sunrise.

It was a beautiful day to go sailing. The sun came up as we tacked hard on the wind past the outer jetty and onto a course heading north. LOW KEY and I were bound for the beach town of Natal just an overnighter away. I had Nessie steering us in light wind as I sailed close-hauled up the coast. I had gone down below to check the e-chart when I thought I heard some yelling. I came up to find us blazing past two poor guys in a wooden rowboat who were fishing at anchor. I watched as their anchor rode slipped, too close, under the keel and past the rudder at five knots. I looked at the guys only a few feet away and motioned that I was sorry. They put on big smiles and waved and seemed to instantly forgive me. I was pissed. I am usually very careful when so close to shore. Lesson learned!

I was running along the 10-meter line at the time, trying to pinch up and head offshore. Offshore wasn't much easier. Just before sunset, I hooked up on one of the nearly invisible crab pot floats. Dropping sail and going for an evening swim didn't seem like fun at the time. Out came the machete. I did my best Tarzan impersonation hanging off the windvane steering gear and hacking away at the monster who was holding us fast to the ocean floor. With a twang, we shot forward and the rest of the line pulled itself free of the boat.

Once again further offshore, I had finally gotten out of range of the floats. Now I was deep in among the fishing fleet. It was super dark and all I could see were tons of lantern lights bobbing all around me. I ducked, I weaved, I jibed, before getting bored with the constant surveillance required. It was approaching my bedtime too. I headed out further. I headed out to the place where I feel the safest, the shipping lanes. No fisherman in his right mind would venture into the lanes. He'd have to be crazy. I slept heavily . . . in between alarms. My radar detector (CARD) signals me to wake up so I can watch the big ships go by. Sometimes I would call them up, just to say hi. There are some interesting people manning the con on those big ships.

New Year's in Natal

The sun came up and I was happy to enter into the log that I hadn't hit anything in 12 hours . . . that I was aware of. I sailed into the port of Natal and took a mooring. I would later be told to put down my anchor and some chain, just in case. I cleaned up LOW KEY and dinghied over to the Belgian boat called MONIKA. Over some frosty beers, Connie and his wife gave me the low down on the Club, checking in and the immediate area. They thought I was British originally. Even after they found out I was from the States, they asked me to stay and have dinner with them—fresh-caught fish of some freaky Amazon variety . . . which was great.

Through the e-mail grapevine (fibervine?), I learned that I had a friend who owned a bar in Natal. I had 24 hours if I was going to find him in time to celebrate New Year's Eve with someone I knew. Wilson owned a place called Gringo's Martini Bar. I walked the local beach in Natal, before finding the cab stand and asking about the bar. The guys thought that Gringo's was most likely in a place called Punta Negra. Let's go. Punta Negra was about 20 minutes away. It's another long beach area, this time with wall-to-wall bars and restaurants. I had some pizza at a nice Italian place—with beer, $8 (feel like I'm rich in places like this). All fueled up, I walked the mile length of the happening strip. I even searched inland some on the advice of another taxi guy, to no avail. I cabbed "home."

It was New Year's Eve. I started with a big breakfast at the Club, served by a waitress I would get to know well. Dina (Dinalva) wanted to practice her English—perfect. I checked the boat in with the Polícia Federal and then got on the wrong bus, which took me back to the local beach. To regroup, I sat down at the shady roadside palapa bar and ordered a coldy. I met some old Brazilian seafarer and his nieces. We talked about foreign ports and told sailor lies (accounts of real events that landlubbers often discount as fabricated). You could tell that it was a big event when Uncle Gustavio was in town. The girls listened intently as the old man told his stories and dispensed his beverage into their little glasses.

And then it was back to Punta Negra to continue the search. If I was unsuccessful, then I would be doomed to spend New Year's Eve in that beautiful town on the water with the very cool, merry-making local population. This time I walked the entire length of the bay. At the north end was a string of large beach homes, many having big private gatherings, some with live music.

Walking back through the central area, I was stopped by a kid (18ish) trying to tempt locals from the strand to sit at his plastic tables and enjoy his chilly beverages. His tables were just off the beach, off to the side of a big stage that was set up to entertain the throngs of revelers. It seemed like the perfect spot to enjoy the festivities. I asked for beer and got it, but the kid insisted that I try the favorite Brazilian cocktail, the Caipirinha. Sure, why not? Now, beer is a good drink for me because you can only drink so much beer at a sitting. On special occasions I tend to get comfortable and drink until the money runs out. With cocktails, this is bad policy, especially in Brazil where running out of money is nearly impossible. I remember enjoying the show and the endless parade of beautiful people traversing the strand and even the incredible fireworks display over the bay at midnight . . . but that's about it.

I awoke to the sun coming up, on the beach, comfortable as can be. I must have had fun. Since I had arrived in Brazil, people kept telling me to not wear jewelry, to leave my camera at my "hotel," and to keep my money out of sight. I don't own jewelry, didn't bring my camera, and when I woke up on that beautiful New Year's morning, I had everything I had the night before (minus about $15, which would amply explain my current fuzziness) plus phone numbers from two girls. I shouldn't be left alone on the holidays. I brushed myself off, bought a stack of beef-on-a-stick from a strand cart, and eased myself into a cab. I holed up for the day, happy and safe back on LOW KEY, and watched movies and ate great hangover food (you know, mac n' cheese, popcorn, beef, etc.) and drank lots of water.

Crew arrival

The rest of the week, I worked on boat projects, did laundry at the club, and cleaned up LOW KEY for my incoming crewmember, Jay. Jay arrived on Friday and I found him at the club bar chatting up my waitress. He said he was just practicing his Portuguese. Dina brought my evening cerveja with a warm smile, and Jay and I talked about cruising and his work and we talked about the passage ahead. We had a 1,400 mile stretch to French Guiana, usually downwind and down current, the kind of passage we like. Back at the boat, we watched *Captain Ron* because (was it possible?) he hadn't seen it.

Jay spent the next day visiting travel agents. He was concerned about flying out of French Guiana when we got there. "I wouldn't worry too much about it, Jay," I told him, "It's French, there is going to be a beautiful airport with international flights." This conversation started a two-week battle of visions. Jay was convinced from reading the online ads for motels in Cayenne that the place was going to be a swamp-ridden string of decrepit villages struggling to make the transition into the 19th century. I maintained, throughout our sail, that the place was going to be the definition of paradise, an incarnation of Eden, a place where French hotties ran topless on the beaches to and from cabanas where they fetched coldies for their thirsty friends from the new world who comfortably lazed in chaise lounges.

That night we attended the dock party with the French, Belgian and Argentinean boats. The evening started with a fishing contest which Jay and I unwittingly entered. The guys were lined up on the dock when we arrived, poles in hand, trying to pull something edible from the river water. As we motored up, a long thin fish flew out of the water and landed in the dinghy. The thing had teeth that were greatly disproportionate to its size and its jaws were a snappin'. I cupped my important parts and instructed Jay to jump out as soon as we hit the dock. I was close behind him. I ambled over to the guys to see how the fishing had been going. "Nothing yet, Woody," said Sapin. I told him our entry was in the dinghy and if he wanted to cook it up he could get it out himself.

Later I brought in my guitar, which I still couldn't play, and they passed it around and sang tunes from all over the world. It was a great night of music, food and good friends. I had finally tracked down the location of the elusive Gringo's Martini Bar and my friend Wilson. As the party dispersed on the dock, we hopped in a cab and ventured back out to Punta Negra. I found my old friend Wilson who set a couple beers in front of us, and we got caught up for a few minutes. He then took us into the backpacker bar area in the valley. We had a great time there, after which Wilson poured us into his car and carted us back to the yacht club. Thanks, dude.

We checked out of the country the next day. It only took about six hours. It was much less painful than the checking-in process in Recife. There was one semi-shady incident. Our taxi driver, a little red-eyed shifty dude, took us the long way to one of the offices, straight through a really bad part of town. He drove through very slowly, honking his horn from time to time. I'm still not sure what he had in mind, but it could have been bad. Jay didn't like it either. I locked the back doors and kept myself within arm's length of the driver. If I was going to buy it in this little backwoods barrio, then I was going to take that driver with me.

Everywhere that I could, I would mail a disk of pictures, and each month I would e-mail my column and feature article out to *Lats & Atts*. Our very talented editor Sue would put everything together and into the magazine. Before departing from Natal, I shot into town to the Internet café to submit the month's articles to *Lats*. Hotmail was down as usual, so I sent my stuff through my new G-mail account. "E-mail Sent" is what the screen said, which I took to mean that my e-mails had been received. Not so, I would find out at my next port o' call, 12 days later. The Mac servers at the office had blocked my e-mail from the new edress. I did finally see the substitution article from Bob and Sue. They put together a couple articles for and about me with some old pictures. It occurs to me that I've got some old pictures that might need digging out!

Ciao Brazil

And finally we said goodbye to our newest, dearest friends and cast off the lines! As I hoisted sail, we drifted into the center of the river and pointed the bow toward the entrance. We had decent breeze (15 knots) and so LOW KEY trucked along making good progress against the incoming tidal current. The entrance to the river was breaking on both sides and rough in the middle. It seemed doable so we plunged into the turmoil, and, finally, sailed out the other side unscathed, into the deep blue and large rolling swell of the open ocean.

Once out we encountered a bunch of small, completely flat fishing sailboats. I had seen these rigs on the beaches. I thought that they were just for show, for the tourists, but here they were being sailed by two and three people on the ocean. At least one of the guys was always standing up, presumably to keep the little boat balanced. Very cool.

Jay seemed to know what he was doing on the boat. He had raced Hobie cats before, so he knew, generally, how to sail and he knew the silly words we use on boats. This all made sailing with him easy. The only thing was, I'm not sure Jay had done much "roughing it." Early on in the trip I heard him say, "All this fresh air is giving me a headache." But he adapted, he overcame. When confronted with showering only every three days he declared, "Baby wipes . . . the best invention since duct tape."

On our first day we logged 147nm, 138nm the second. We had over a knot of current pushing us along and decent wind, mostly aft. I had the big sail up, the original version of the sail that now lies at the bottom of the Indian Ocean. The sail is so old that it is brown, but since it won't die, I won't replace it. It was starting to chafe where it slid along the bow pulpit, so I sewed on a patch.

Jay mentioned that, in among the totally putrid swamps, the European rocket launching facility, Arianespace, was in French Guiana. Trying to sway things in a positive direction and to pass the time, I suggested that there would also then be hot Euro rocket scientist babes with French accents and low cut lab coats that had pencil protectors with lollipops in 'em, eh? Why not!

Jay and I had started the watch game where points are gained by spotting stuff on or off your watch. I spotted a whale, two points since you don't see whales that often. This whale looked like a giant dolphin (Beluga?). And then there were two and then three. . . . In the next hour we must have seen a hundred surf by the boat. They were obviously on their way somewhere since they were moving pretty fast. They would come zooming down from windward. When a swell would peak up, they would shoot up into the crest and surf along, their large bulbous nose poking out the front. It was very cool to see them but it was a little unnerving too. They were so huge and moving so fast, so close to the boat. Some would break off to have a look. They would duck under the boat and shoot up along side, never breaking the surface. Again, gigantic and a little close for comfort—but beautiful nonetheless.

We crossed the equator that night. I know, I'm supposed to get dressed up and make Jay pay homage to Neptune, cover him in entrails and make him eat bad food, etc . . . I really couldn't be bothered. I thought about throwing him overboard and making him swim across the equator, but it was nighttime and I didn't want to have to make that phone call to his girlfriend if Jay got lost. We decided that he would drink a warm beer. This would be a bonus to the equator crossing for me, but for Jay, who had already suffered the realization that the boat didn't have air-conditioning, it seemed like punishment enough.

Jay mentioned the unlikely possibility of him finding a hotel with air-conditioning in all of Cayenne. "Jay!" I said, "I heard that Travel Magazine refers to French Guiana as the Paris of the Caribbean, South America's French Riviera, the Cote d'Azure de Sur," and on and on till Jay only had pretty pictures in his head.

Would you believe . . .

The next day Jay called me on deck. "What the hell is that?" he asked. I expected to see more whales or a funny-lookin' ship. Jay had spotted a waterspout dead ahead. It had just touched down. I dove for the camera and got a couple of not so brilliant shots. "You gonna keep sailing right at it?" Jay asked. Good question. It didn't look that dangerous. But then, my idea of what constitutes danger had been downgraded over the last year or so. The waterspout veered and left us.

I let some weather sneak up on us, just after dark. The wind kicked up and we had a proper squall like I hadn't seen since Mexico, 18 months before. I had the big ancient sail poled out, which is not what you want in 30 knots and building. We had to run like dogs. Unless conditions absolutely demand it, I don't like to run. It just keeps you under the bad weather for longer, often moving in the wrong direction. Somehow I got the big sail down without ripping it. I triple reefed the main and pointed us back on course. Eight sail changes later, the front passed and the sun came up, leaving us a little tired. It was good, I thought, for Jay to experience some proper weather on what was otherwise a good, fast, downwind leg.

Jay was still reading up on Cayenne. He read that the launch site crews went to Devil's Island and played volleyball when they weren't working. "See!" I said as I easily conjured up rocket scientist babes playing bikini VB for Jay. I didn't stop there. I created a plan for us to tell vacationing Euro chicks at the bars of Cayenne that we were astronauts preparing to go up on a dangerous mission on the next launch. Chicks would certainly go for that.

Looking back, the leg from Natal to Cayenne contained some pretty interesting natural phenomena. I was on my early morning watch. The wind was down and the sea was pretty calm. The boat was sailing along at 4.5 knots. I was reading in the cockpit, trying to ignore another amazing sunrise, when I heard a rushing sound in the air. It sounded a little like a waterfall. A vision of that painting of the ships falling off the edge of the world floated through my head. I continued reading while my mind chewed on the issue. We were too far out for surf, there was no detected ship radar, and besides, I had just done my 360 degree horizon scan. What could it be, rain? There were no clouds in the sky. The sound got downright loud and so I gave up guessing and stood to have a look. Up ahead the water was roiling. It looked like a giant fish boil, but the turbulence was in a straight line, as far as the eye could see. I had just been looking at the chart. It could not possibly be a reef—we were a hundred miles offshore. It turned out to be the granddaddy of current lines. As we sailed through it, I noticed that the water changed from blue to green. We had just sailed into the outflow of the Amazon. I had read that you could drink the water in front of the great river, 50 miles out to sea. That far out the water was still fresh.

The sailing was perfect that day, not super fast, but very smooth. At night you could see both the Southern Cross and the North Star and, of course, the Seven Sisters, who have always looked after me.

"Hey, Jay, do you know what the French word for party is? Cayenne, dude!"

On approach

It was nighttime, there were little islands between Cayenne's entrance channel and us, there was a squall bearing down, and the approach lights seemed backward to me. Hmmmm, sounds like a perfect time to enter a river harbor I've never been into. As we got closer, it started to make sense. The chart I bought in South Africa showed the lights arrayed in the system used by most of the world (outside the U.S.) of red left returning. The lights we were seeing were clearly arranged red right returning. I suppose, if you looked directly through the Earth from South Africa to Cayenne, the reds would be on the left. With that problem solved, we sailed around the little islands and headed LOW KEY up the center of the channel. With arrival coldies in hand, the wind and rain from the squall hit us—it happens. What I was not prepared for was the amazing side current that was sweeping us out of the channel. I had to point the boat 45 degrees to port to keep us lined up. Being French, the channel was wide and overly lit with markers about every 100 yards. The funny thing was that it was only about 10 feet deep in most places. And this was their main port. We sailed in as far as we could, and when the wind died, we pulled off to the side and dropped the hook. Exhausted, we went to sleep. It is always great to have the boat safely parked after a long haul and get that first long night's sleep.

"There's a marina with a clubhouse and over here is a resort with Hobie Cats." This is what I heard coming from the deck at sunrise as I fought to sleep in, just a little. Hadn't I just sailed like a thousand miles? It was my turn to be cynical.

"Dude, this is Guiana! There is nothing here but swamps, bugs and tribal ghettos!"

CHAPTER 19

Parlez vous Anglais?

After sailing the 1,400 mile leg from Natal, Brazil to Cayenne, French Guiana, my crew Jay and I found ourselves anchored safely inside the mouth of the Mahury River. The place was really beautiful, lush and green. We upped anchor and motored deeper inland. I didn't have a cruising guide to French Guiana (who does?) but I had heard that there was a small marina up river. Just past the ship quay we found the docks. They were full of local boats, but a guy on the dock motioned us to side-tie to a powerboat. I tried to get some local info from the guy, but when he discovered that we didn't speak French he walked away.

A young couple who was preparing their boat for cruising helped us out with some check-in information. She said that the Port Captain came down to the docks every few days if I wanted to wait. Pretty casual governmental situation—the way we like it. Jay had to start looking for flights out of Cayenne, and I was looking forward to moving on to Trinidad, so I decided to jump-start the process. I walked up the road to the Port Captain's office. Young Oliver helped me with the port paperwork. There was a port fee, which had to be paid in Euros. Of course, I had no Euros yet and town was 20 miles away. Over at the cashier's office there was a discussion, in French, and a phone call was made. Early in the process, I noticed that Oliver had pulled out some of his own money. They quickly sorted it out and Oliver walked me outside. He explained that my port fees had been waived and that France welcomes their friends from the United States. How nice was that?

I walked over to Customs. The big, roly-poly Customs guy laughed at me. He explained, in broken English, that this was a shipping port and that Customs doesn't deal with little boats. Cool! As I walked out, he told me that if I wanted to help out, I could marry a fat girl and take her home with me. French comedy—no extra charge. Immigration, same story (without the incongruous joking), they didn't want to see me either. I love the EU!

You have a problem with French people? Come to French Guiana. I walked into a shipping office to ask about a bus into Cayenne. Micheline was just taking off for lunch and offered me a ride to town. Beautiful. Time was limited and Jay was waiting to go to the airport, so I hit the ATM and did a quick check of e-mail. Jay almost lost me for the afternoon at this point. Sitting in the Victorian-era building under a cool fan, with fast Internet and a coldy, I was pretty happy. I kept it quick though and then hopped into a cab. Normally I would find a bus, but I figured this was the best way to get a cab out to our "marina" in the sticks. 20 Euros to the boat (almost $30). Wow. I collected Jay and we headed for the airport. While I wandered about, Jay discovered that the airline that went where he wanted to go had gone out of business while we were at sea. We would have to find him other means of travel.

Our trip to the airport wasn't fruitless—Jay rented a car! We drove back to town, and Jay continued the search for an escape route. He checked online, went to two different travel agents, and on and on. I hung out in my new favorite place—the old school, brew-friendly Internet/bar/Austrian restaurant. Jay got a room that night at the Hotel Bodega in town. We made big plans to take real showers, hit the town and stay out late. By the time I got out of the shower, Jay was passing out in front of the TV. I went out solo as usual.

Jay was up early and out the door. By noon, with the help of some semi-shady locals, he had formulated a plan. The French had never built a road to Brazil, presumably to keep the flow of Brazilians into their little paradise to a minimum. Legend had it that there was a dirt road that, when not flooded out, went all the way to the edge of the Oiapoque River—the border with Brazil. Jay had arranged transport to the river via small car. From there, the generally accepted jungle hearsay was that he would be able to hire a canoe to deliver him across the great river so he could hitch a ride to a town where a bus would take him to the nearest small airport. Suffice to say that I have heard from him since, and his story proves that the truth can be more amazing than fiction.

I was crewless once again. Back at the dock, I untied the lines and drifted out with the two-knot current. Free from land with its bugs and hot air, I sheeted hard and pointed high to give myself some distance from shore. Being five degrees north, I was in the ITCZ, often referred to as the doldrums. For me, near land, the area was a squally mess. I had good wind most of the time so I was going fast, but then it would go calm and I would know that I was about to get slammed. During one such event, the wind hit and I found myself running in 30+ knots with a full main and headsail. Nessie doesn't like running with a full main, and so the boat rounded up, hard. I woke up and came out on deck to find the boat on its ear dragging sideways. I had a couple words with Nessie, we don't always get along, and took the helm. It was too much for me, too. It was kind of funny. There I was fighting the tiller with all my strength trying to keep the boat straight, lightning all around, white water spewing across the cockpit. It reminded me of that movie *Dove* with the Graham kid who was constantly in the cockpit getting his ass handed to him in various weather situations during his circumnavigation. How come on my trip around the world I never got beat up in the cockpit with the boat out of control before? As I finally emerged from my sleepy stupor, I realized that all I had to do was shorten sail. I took the main down, the helm went light again and Nessie took over. I went back to sleep as LOW KEY zoomed comfortably along at top speed. The "just keep the boat balanced" lesson was re-learned.

Once clear of the ITCZ, I had big wind just aft of the beam

and good current. I realized then why not many cruisers make the slog from El Carib to Brazil. Going the easy direction, I was having 140- to 150-mile days. With all that wind, the wind generator was putting out big amps. We like that because all the toys become available—the refer running full-time, smailing through SailMail, and listening to the BBC on the big radio were no longer luxuries.

During the quick 600-mile run to Tobago, I had a chance to pickle the watermaker. I love the watermaker, but I had to run the thing every few days to keep it clean. I had completed my last ocean crossing for awhile, and with the rest of my route laced with good water sources, I wouldn't be needing it. Pickled, it can sit unused for a year.

I should mention here that I had been struggling for a while with the Big Question. This was my turning point. Tobago sits at the bottom of the beautiful island chain we often refer to as the Caribbean. I could so easily just linger and spend another year thoroughly exploring the islands before making my way to the canal and back up to California. It was a really tough call. I decided to continue as planned, taking some solace in the fact that I'd surely return.

It was the evening of my fourth day out that I spotted the glow of Tobago on the horizon ahead. That meant that Trinidad, my ultimate destination, was off to port, just over the horizon. Trinidad and Tobago are one nation. I pulled into Tobago first because it was closer and I wanted to check in before the weekend to avoid overtime fees. As I approached Scarborough, I had to take the sails down. I didn't want to arrive before 9:00 am, also to avoid overtime fees. I'm sure LOW KEY was confused with this. I usually indulge her craving to arrive at night. As it turns out, no one in Tobago cared.

And finally the Caribbean

As I closed with the coast and cleaned up, I listened to a local radio station. There was a female DJ doing the intros to the songs. I was loving the accent; that cute, singsong flow of words—even if I couldn't always understand it. A public service announcement came on that at first sounded very important. "Doen put more than 15 feet 6 inches on your carnival vehicle. Alllso, it is ellegal to lift the lectrical wires with poles to pass unda-dem." Oh ya, it's Carnival time.

I went into town to check in. I was a little concerned because I didn't get the all-important Zarpe, the country clearance form from French Guiana that all nations expect to see before letting you into their country. Both the Port Captain and Immigration asked for it and both times I told them French Guiana doesn't do it. Both times the official just looked away uncomfortably and skipped to the next question. It was unbelievable. With French Guiana dissing the obviously stupid and outdated clearance procedure, the whole global check-in façade could disintegrate! It's happening in Europe you know. No check-ins between countries. Imagine the consequences. There will be hoards of jobless officials walking the streets of what once were clearance ports with an ink stamp in one hand and an empty cup in the other, pleading pathetically, "Clearance fees—have you paid your clearance fees?"

Back in the anchorage, I spent the rest of the day drinking coldies on ZIPOLOTE with Holcom from Norway. Young Holcom was cruising on a budget. His rig was pretty low end. Still, that didn't stop him from enjoying ice cold beers. He had no refer onboard. He had one of those cheap-ass foam coolers that fit perfectly in a spot on his cockpit floor. You could tell the thing had had some use. It was grimy and of a design that I was pretty sure they had done away with sometime in the '70s. Holcom said he had a deal with the water/ice guy directly ashore. Whatever it was, the beer was always frosty when I stopped by ZIPOLOTE.

I went into town for pizza one night with Holcom. We were minding our own business in the mostly empty pizza parlor when eight mostly blonde girls walked in. We didn't think it was strange at first—we're both used to seeing flocks of blondes where we are from. So we decided to bet on their country of origin. "English?" Holcom started with. "No, further north" I countered. And then it hit me. "Dude, they're totally Norwegian," which was, by coincidence, where Holcom was from. We walked over to one of the tables, found out they were from Norway, and Holcom went into a long conversation in Norwegian. They were in town to play some sport—cricket or curling or something—and they were on a pretty tight leash, which became evident when the crotchety caretaker woman showed up and stole our hard earned girls.

I left for Trinidad late that night so I could arrive the next day. To get to Chaguaramas, the cruising anchorage in Trinidad, you sail 24 miles across a channel and continue down the mostly uninhabited north side of the island before hooking around the west end. It was a beautiful night for a sail. The moon was almost full and the warm wind was aft. By about half way across the channel as I passed by low sections of the high north side of Trinidad, I started to hear a deep thrumming beat. Carnival was on!

Just before dawn I went by the space shuttle launch pad heading to windward. Well, that's what I thought it was at first. It turned out to be a giant oil rig-looking thing, all lit up and being towed by four oversized tug boats. I woke up just in time. I almost sailed into the front of that mess. It would have taken me weeks to get untangled. I called the tugs on the radio, no answer.

It was a perfect day as I sailed into the lush green mountain pass that protects the northwest approach to Chaguaramas Bay. Arriving at the same time was a really cool looking sailing boat called VISUAL NOTE from Belem, Brazil. I had never seen anything like this boat. It was all dark varnished wood. The boat had a proud prow and rib-looking planks supporting the cabin roof. It was a floating work of art. Suffice to say that you don't see many cruisers like that one.

The check-in at Chaguaramas was easy, with all the offices right next to each other. Come to think of it, I don't think I've ever seen that before. Port Captain, Immigration and Customs are never in the same area. I know that the Mexicans, for example, go to great lengths to make sure the offices are on opposite sides of town, if not in different towns altogether. O.K., enough bureaucracy bashing . . . for now.

I anchored, launched the dinghy and headed straight up to the Crew's Inn Restaurant for coldies and a fat Caesar salad. Chaguaramas was a nice place—a complete cruising community. Everything a cruiser could want was there. Along the bay there were marinas, haul out yards (to 200 tons), chandleries, cruisy bars and restaurants, Internet places and banks with ATMs. There were sailmakers, mechanics, electricians, welders and prop specialists. Anything marine related, you could get done. In the mornings, there was the most complete cruisers' net I've ever heard (0800, channel 68). The steep jungle ridge with birds and howler monkeys was across the street. On the downside, Chag is next to a giant city and we know what that means: guaranteed crime. Anchorages next to cities never keep me around for long.

Cruising art

In the afternoon, I went over to check out that great boat that I sailed in with. Yuri, a German painter, built VISUAL NOTE by hand on the jungly banks of the Amazon outside a little town called Belem. The wood was hewn out of the jungle by the river, and was comprised of that magic, super-oily, unrottable variety. Even the turnbuckles were handmade by Yuri from stainless rod. It was unbelievable. While building his incredible boat, Yuri made the acquaintance of young Rosie. When his vessel was finished, he packed up his things and Rosie (I believe there was some compensation to the family in the form of livestock), and they put to sea.

I spent the afternoons of the next two days over at VISUAL NOTE rearranging their anchors. The boat was a little too close to shore. Yuri was having some problems with the engine and planned on being anchored there a while, so we decided to get him set up properly. There were no winches aboard VN—hard to hand-make a winch, I guess—and so lifting the two 100-pound anchors was a challenge, especially once they had dug in. I brought LOW KEY over the second day to use her winches to ease the process. In Trinidad, Yuri has found the perfect place, and in VISUAL NOTE, the perfect gallery to showcase his art. I'm sure he'll be there for a while, so be sure to drop by and say hello.

I had been having problems with my little prehistoric Volvo overheating. Happily parked in a place where I had access to parts (and mechanics if I really screwed it up), I tore apart the exhaust manifold and gave it a thorough cleaning, slapped it back together and fired her up. Purred like a kitten lying in the shade.

While in Chaguaramas, I checked out all the chandleries (*Lats & Atts* was sold out everywhere) and boats in the yards and partook of the many cruiser hangouts. I took a maxi (a very full minivan taxi/bus) and headed into town for a haircut/fast food/movie day. Back in Chag, I dropped off old oil and three old batteries I never really used at one of the boatyards. I was not even a customer and they helped me carry the batteries—just nice people all over.

At 0600 on my last full day in Trinidad, I moved LOW KEY into a berth in the Coral Cove Marina. I know, way outa character, but I had crew coming. As I went to park, I could hear music wafting through the hills. It was coming from one of the giant raves still going on from the night before. Shoot, missed another one. Trinidad was the first place in over a year that had 110-volt power at the dock that I could plug into (usually Euro 220-volt). I cranked up the refer (coldies), hooked up the battery charger, washed down the boat and filled the water tanks. Then I rigged up the hammock and slithered in, doing my best to blend in with the other fat-cat marina-cruisers.

Rick and Gretchen arrived around 1600. I welcomed them aboard and showed them around. Rick was an electrical contractor and young Gretchen was a physical therapist. They had come from Northern Indiana. We talked about what was going on in the midwest and how my trip was going, so far. Later, we headed out in the dinghy to find the bar/restaurant that was hosting the Super Bowl, a very foreign event there in Carnival country. There was no room inside, so we ate on the deck overlooking the bay. When the game started, the wait staff opened the big windows and we ended up with great seats to the game. The game was good and all, but I mostly wanted to see the commercials. Unfortunately, the satellite feed was from Mexico, so I just got to see the same Chevy commercial 10 or 15 times.

In the morning we started the check-out procedure. A little problem developed at Immigration. I did not have some stamped piece of paper they needed. The lady started getting short with me. There were no options to replace it. If it couldn't be found I could not check out of the country. They make a big deal about letting you into these countries and then they threaten you with making you stay. I found the paper among my crew lists. The Tobago Immigration lady had stamped one of my crew lists instead of the all important Trinidad-Tobago form. This lady wasn't having it though. She decided she needed to call the Tobago lady to confirm all was well. The Tobago Immigration office would not be open for two days. I hung in there and never stopped smiling and being gracious. I think it wore her down. She finally cracked a smile herself and stamped our passports.

I took my new friends to VISUAL NOTE for a look and so I could say goodbye to Yuri and Rosie. Yuri informed me that because VN would be staying put for a while, young Rosie had decided that she wanted to continue on with LOW KEY. I thought about asking Yuri what he wanted for her, but my boat was already pretty full, and so it was not to be.

Carnival

Gretchen, Rick and I took a bus into town. The Carnival debauchery was in full swing. The streets were packed with people and makeshift stands along the route, selling food and coldies. Big diesel flatbed trucks were loaded up with generators, commercial coolers, mini bars, dancers, sound systems and giant speakers—mostly speakers of the six- to eight-foot variety. The sound these trucks created was unbelievable. You felt the music waves hit you. Some of the sound systems were so powerful, I swear I could see the music. And it got you moving. Which was what everyone was doing. Each truck represented a tribe, I learned, and each tribe had a different glittery showgirl costume. There were 30 or 40 people, mostly women, dressed up and dancing around their truck as it crawled through the streets. We watched the parade of bands, DJs and flesh for two hours and never saw the same truck twice. There must have been a hundred tribes.

Trinidad was a good stop. Carnival is a must-see on the Caribbean tour, and the cruising facilities at Chaguaramas were comprehensive. Contrary to what I had heard, the locals were all great to me, even downtown. On the negative side is the 15% VAT (sales tax) and the $160 worth of check-out fees—a new world record for LOW KEY, with Brazil and American Samoa close behind.

Maybe it wasn't the best way to break in the new crew to their first offshore passage, but as it worked out, we took off at night with no moon. You couldn't see a thing. No matter, I had plotted our track carefully on the GPS. All we had to do was follow the line, which was made more challenging by an impressive cross current. I had a hard time explaining that even though the flashing light was currently on our port side, we would surely leave it to starboard. As soon as we were clear of the inner bay (far as I could tell), I hoisted sail and shut down the engine. It was a beautiful night—you could hear the crickets. We were sheltered from the swell by the other islands. We sailed west before turning up to sail between Chacachacare and Huevos Islands, the last Trinidad-Tobago islands before Venezuela. After clearing Boca de Navios, we were in the open sea. Our destination: Dutch Bonaire of the ABC islands.

On the advice of a Trinidad marina-cruiser, we sailed across the top of Venezuela with our nav lights off! He was telling us that "lights out" was the only way to avoid pirates. I was not a fan of the idea, but at the time I was responsible for more than just myself. Mostly I took the advice because if I hadn't and we had to return to Trinidad, pirated, I would have had to hear the pirate expert say, "I told you so." On the positive side, LOW KEY was fully crewed and could keep proper watches.

My crew were expecting a pretty easy sail. The pilot charts showed the leg as an easy down wind, down current, run. It was easy going that first day. The next day the wind piped up and swung around onto the beam. Before I knew it, we were triple reefed and things were getting pretty salty. The kids were good about it.

Kralendijk (yikes) is the main town on Bonaire and is located on the west side of the island. We arrived at night, three days later, and sailed south around the reefs. We motored up to Kralendijk and took a mooring. In Bonaire, the entire island is a nature preserve and so there is no anchoring. Bonaire is one of those great stops where you arrive at night and wake up in the morning to find your boat parked in perfect water over white sand. We dinghied over to the boat IRISH EYES from Michigan. It was Eric and Colleen's first season. They were very cheery and helpful with much needed local info. I offered to come by later to help them set up their computer for cruising.

The island check-in was quick. Customs and Immigration were Euro easy (and free, as they should be in a civilized country). It was the cutest town you ever saw, clean and well laid out. The ATMs dispensed your choice of Gildas or U.S. dollars. We had a big lunch at one of the seaside cafés and retired to LOW KEY for a swim. With help, I gave LOW KEY's bottom a quick once over cleaning. A little later I dropped the kids ashore for the evening. Back at the boat, I strung up the hammock and kicked back with a coldy and some tunes to help get me through another stellar sunset in paradise.

Gretchen and Rick left in the morning. It was Saturday, so I moved the boat to a mooring closer to the Quay (little party pier) off the center of the village. At the end of the Quay was a mini bar. Legend had it that Saturday was a big night at Karel's

Bar . . . and it was. I try to stay close to the action, you know, for your sake, the reader.

Crew eh?

I had another crew member flying in, a young Canadian lass who had just finished medical school and was taking a break before starting her internship. I wasn't sure exactly when to expect her. I was at the hostel/restaurant/bar/Internet place checking my e-mail when some hottie walked through, as they do in a backpacker/diver paradise like Bonaire. The poor girl was asking the guy at the front desk if he had heard from the airline about her lost bag. The poor girl had the same last name as my new crew. I logged out and caught up to Angelina in the Hostel. We had Mexican food on the waterfront and a couple drinks at the Quay before going back to check out the boat.

With her bag missing, Ange found herself ill-equipped for island life, and so the next day we went bikini shopping—the things we do for our crew! When we returned to the boat, I could see that someone had been aboard. I had almost forgotten. Ange let me know in one of her e-mails that she was into diving. When I was aboard IRISH EYES, I mentioned that my new crew was going to want to dive. For helping them with the computer stuff—well, my cockpit was full of their dive gear and four full tanks. Perfect! The best dive spot on the island was reported to be just around the corner of the nearest islet. Ange and I drifted off the mooring and sailed the couple miles to a mooring over the dive spot. We had it to ourselves. With warm sunny weather and clear water conditions, we did two amazing dives that day before returning to the village, the sun setting behind us—a perfect day.

We met Jay and his girlfriend Jani in town that night for dinner and drinks. That's right, the same Jay from the French Guiana to Brazil border crossing adventure. After completing his jungle mission, he decided to bring his girlfriend down to

Bonaire to do some diving and to get her a sailing lesson. In town, Jay decided he wanted to do a pub-crawl, which was a funny thing to want to do in a three-pub town. We ended up back at the Quay, of course, where Ange, who was an ex-bartender, introduced us to the Flaming Sambuca. After you pour this noxious, highly flammable concoction into your gullet, a friend (?) follows it with a lit match. The whole thing ignites, much to the horror of innocent Dutch vacationers walking by.

Jay picked us up in the morning (no, it wasn't early) and drove us to the airport. They had Ange's bag. Yea! In good spirits we went with Jay and Jani on an island tour. We saw lizards and cactus and well kept roads. Jay dropped us back at the Quay.

Ange and I were fired up to start our sail to Cartegena. We prepped the boat and motored over to the marina, nice place. I fueled LOW KEY while Ange hung out on deck and looked good, much to the dismay of the babeless dudes on the big-dough motoryacht aft of us who probably already had good reasons to not like blow boaters. We enjoyed Ange-made pizza as we sailed west on the calm lee waters of the bay before poking our bow out to start the hard reach to Colombia.

CHAPTER 20

Sailing the Southern Caribbean

Our stay in Dutch Bonaire, the B of the ABCs, was incredible. Good people, clean land and water and world class diving made for a great cruising stop. Ange and I were now headed for the San Blas Islands off Panama. We had talked about stopping in Cartegena, Colombia. I had heard great things about the place. My only concern was exposing young Ange to the threat of piracy off the shores of Colombia. We talked about the pros and cons that first day out of Bonaire. She was as fired up as I was to take the risks. We decided that we would not be bypassing Cartegena.

The sailing was fast and pretty comfortable . . . at first. A couple days into our five-day rip across the top of South America, it started to get bumpy. The pilot charts I had onboard showed this reach to be pretty mellow. That's what I told Ange to expect. While in Bonaire, I had downloaded some info on cruising Colombia. It turns out that it is pretty much common knowledge that the southern Caribbean can get rough . . . and it did. To avoid the coastal areas, we sailed offshore which meant we had to endure a long twelve-hour beam reach to get back to land. You know the drill. Carving along between 20-foot breaking swells that roll over the boat from time to time. Ange held up well considering that she hadn't done much sailing.

The seas mellowed as we approached the coast. We sailed

down along the peninsula that protects Cartegena. We found the entrance and powered in. It was a black night lit only by the city lights. The buoys were hard to follow, and so twice I had to blindly follow my GPS line to find the next buoy. I had bought the harbor chart in Bonaire, but it didn't say where the small boat anchorage was. In the inner harbor we found masts. We pulled up to a boat with a guy in the cockpit. The boat was from Canada, which was fine because I had an interpreter (yep, both only spoke English).

There were two marinas. One was real upscale. We opted to put the hook down in front of the other, the Club Nautico. Once again LOW KEY had conquered the sea and safely delivered her crew to another incredible location, this time the beautiful city of Cartegena. It was time for a mini celebration. What do salt-soaked sailors want to do upon arrival in port? Well lotsa stuff, but first—naked, fresh-water deck showers by the low glow of the late night city lights, arrival coldies close by.

The next morning Ange and I took the dink over and met a couple of our fellow cruisers anchored nearby. Richard and Chris, a couple of British gentlemen, gave us the low down of the Club, the check-in process and a quick intro to this end of Cartegena. First things first, we continued in and had breakfast at the club. And after over a year without it, I got to hear Spanish again. I never thought that I'd miss it. Before breakfast was over I had met with my agent (the only way to check into Colombia) and he put me on the phone with the U.S. born Club manager who welcomed us. When I tried to pay for breakfast, I found that they had already started me a club tab. I decided I liked this place. This little "yacht club" was more on top of things than a five-star hotel (not that I would know).

We had a great few days in Cartegena. It is a beautiful city with no obvious crime. Usually I dress down to explore town, but in Cartegena I felt comfortable walking around in my tourist clothes and taking pictures with the digital. The old Spanish architecture is beautiful. The historic town is laced with old homes, little shops and cafés. The city comes complete with its own giant fortress on top of a downtown hill.

On our last night we ventured into the walled city. We checked out the shops and had a drink at a café followed by a perfect dinner at Pelikanos where they had a cruiser's special— a great meal with all you can drink wine. Ange wanted to check out the famous Santa Clara Hotel. We sat down for a drink there in the lush courtyard surroundings after which we played with one of the resident toucans. It was late but before leaving the old town, we stopped by a little hole-in-the-wall. You know how it is. You're walking down some cobblestone street in a foreign town and you hear merrymaking coming from an open door and window. You peer in and some local wanting you to feel comfortable in his part of the world welcomes you in. We partied with a bunch of hilarious people, language not being much of a barrier after all.

Home of the Kuna Indians

But eventually, it was time to leave Cartegena, with a vow to someday return to that beautiful city. We drifted down the long bay and enjoyed a nice pasta dinner before pulling up the sails and shooting out through the pass. Our destination? The San Blas Islands, legendary for their little natives, beautiful water and South Pacific-like coral islands.

Early the next afternoon, we sailed into the Hollandaise Islands in San Blas. We motored up to the area where the other cruising boats had parked. Most of them were anchored over a shelf that looked really shallow. As we pulled alongside one of them, I had to ask how deep it was over there. Fifteen feet? It looked like about four. You gotta love perfect water over white sand. I had explained to young Ange about the beauty of the San Blas Islands, but still she seemed amazed. Parked in perfect water between South Seas islands, we jumped overboard for a swim. Shortly after pulling ourselves from the warm turquoise, we were invited to an island sundowner with the other cruisers. We followed that with popcorn and a movie back on LOW KEY.

The next day I considered doing some light work on the boat. Fortunately, Dennis, a friend from Cartegena, distracted us with an invite to visit his big yacht, VALHALLA, for "a beer." Dennis was from the States. He had sailed into Cartegena years ago on his own boat and decided to stay. He later "acquired" the Formosa 65, VALHALLA, which he used to smuggle backpackers from Cartegena to the San Blas and back. To make this trip via land would mean crossing the notorious Darien Gap, a stretch of terra infested with cocaine plantations and their associated guerilla warriors. We spent the rest of the afternoon and evening enjoying grand VALHALLA and her mostly backpacker crew.

We awoke the next morning and VALHALLA was gone. It was almost time for Ange to start her trek back to Canada. We sailed over to Porvenir, a tiny sand spit of an island with an air strip that had cheap flights to the west coast of Panama where the big airport was. After anchoring yet again in beautiful water, a large dinghy pulled up. It was VALHALLA's. We were informed that Customs was awaiting our arrival. We took our dink ashore and walked into the small customs building next to the air strip. Dennis was behind the desk drinking a coldy. One of the customs agents offered me one while Dennis, all official like, asked to see my papers. It seemed that Dennis was not only well connected in Cartegena, he had friends here too. Needless to say, our check-in to Panama went smoothly.

As it turned out, the President of Panama was in the area, which would explain the large military presence. His huge motoryacht was parked behind us. Ange and I were on LOW KEY eating mac n' cheese when the President's yacht tender pulled up to the little dock ashore. Twenty minutes later, he boarded a large helicopter and took off. That evening we would have to listen while Dennis recounted how he met the President and got a nice picture of himself and the President sitting in the helicopter. Dennis is one of those people who is always in the right place at the right time.

The next morning, I put Ange on a tiny plane and she flew

away. Usually I'm excited to get back to singlehanding. This time it took a couple of days. Back in the anchorage, I met Alex. We had exchanged e-mails a couple of times. He was a fan of *Latitudes & Attitudes* and figured he would be in the San Blas when I was. Alex maintains a website on his cruising adventures at www.projectbluesphere.com. I was finishing up my trip and he was just starting out, and so . . . I gave him my watermaker in exchange for a Max-Prop (folding low-drag propeller) that he wasn't going to use.

I left Porvenir late that afternoon. The island was one of those places where the water was so clear that you constantly think you are going aground even though you are in 30 feet of water. I felt my way around the long reef in the waning light and pointed the bow toward Colón (say ko-lone), home to the Carib side of the Panama Canal.

The next morning, as I closed in on the big port, I found myself surrounded by huge ships all converging on one of the largest shipping hubs on the planet. It was a beautiful day as I sailed through the breakwall and entered the port. My arrival in Colón was a major milestone of my sailing endeavor to circle the earth. Motoring by the world's largest moving objects, I felt euphoric. No matter how far these behemoths had come, they had nothing on me.

The transit shuffle

I parked stern-to-the-quay at the Panama Canal Yacht Club, one of my favorite harbor hangouts. Colón is a great place to hang out . . . for about three days. It is notorious for its 50% unemployment, general thievery and car fires in the streets. I started the process of getting through the canal immediately. That's not true. I actually started the process before I got to Colón. Other cruisers in the Caribbean had been telling me about how it was taking boats three weeks to get a transit date. I had crew flying in on both sides of the canal. I had 10 days max to transit. I started by hiring an agent, via e-mail, while I was in San Blas. I hired Enrique Plummer, a popular Panama agent specializing in transits, though he could get you almost anything in Panama.

Now that I was finally in Colón, I hit the shore running. After a quick shower, mmmm, I taxied to town. At Immigration I called Enrique. It seems I was a little ahead of myself. Enrique said he could have taken care of that for me. Oh well, we were already ahead of the game. Enrique came down to the Club to meet me. I gave him $1,450 cash to cover the transit fee, his fee, lines rental and the large canal deposit. The deposit is in case you wreck the canal somehow. Enrique informed me that my admeasure date, the day when they come down and officially measure your boat, was the next day. Most boats were taking three to four days to get measured. We were on track.

Every night, after being available to aid the transit process, I would meet up with my new cruising friends back at the club. The PCYC is a classic old school pub and restaurant that serves beer and food cheap. The actual bar is shaped like a boat. With walking into town at night not an option, it was great to have the old place at our disposal. I met the boat boys. These were local six-foot-plus men that helped out around the docks of the yacht club. They could sell you tire fenders, rent you lines or line handlers, suggest a laundry or a taxi and generally find you anything. These guys valued their position at the club and didn't take kindly to competition. As the story goes . . . a German cruiser was renting himself out to other boats as a line handler. He was undercutting the boys. After ignoring a warning, our German friend found himself roughed up. He moved on.

One of the cruisers I hung out with was 20-something James. He was helping an older female cruiser with the Caribbean part of her dream of sailing around the world. Against the advice of some of our fellow cruisers, James and I decided to find out what Colón had to offer in terms of nightlife. We cabbed to a couple of places and partied with the locals. Our last stop was the big casino. I introduced James to blackjack. We made it home with $12 profit.

I had arrived on the first. On my fourth day in Colón I got the news that my transit date was on the 15th. That wasn't good enough. Enrique made some calls. He had it changed to the 8th . . . perfect. I had received some e-mails about a new cruiser's TV show that Bob was doing called *Latitudes & Attitudes TV*. He wanted to send a crew down to film LOW KEY's transit. Cool. I called the *Latitudes & Attitudes* office to let them know my transit date and when to expect my next set of writings. The film crew's schedule would be full up that week, so they would have to try to catch up with me at a later date. Word got around at the office that I was on the phone, and, one by one, I got to talk to everyone. It's good to be loved.

My canal crewmember had arrived. Phil was from Texas originally and living in southern Colorado. He owned a dude ranch and offered me a week on the ranch in exchange for a ride through the canal. Sounded good to me. Phil was a classic cowboy. I commented on his cool hat lanyard. "It's a stampede string," I was cordially corrected.

We moved the boat out to the Flats, the area cordoned off for the anchored cruising fleet. We installed cleats as required (my plan to sail around the world without installing the cleats was foiled) and generally prepped the boat for her transit. On transit day we had an old local dude on a surfboard clean the bottom and the prop for a fast slippery run through the canal. Enrique had provided us with four 120-foot lines and my new friends, the boat boys, had sold me a couple of extra fenders. To transit the canal, a boat is required to have four line handlers aboard besides the skipper. I had Phil and was able to get James just as he was leaving his other ride. I did not want to pay for my last two line handlers ($200) and so I checked the yacht club and shanghaied Richard and Jeti. The couple had intended to transit with another, much better appointed, boat but could not wait for their transit date to come. This was their last chance and so they agreed to transit with little low-end LOW KEY. As it turned out, Richard wrote for *Sail*

Magazine. I figured sailing with me would be a good experience for him.

The big ditch

Our canal advisor boarded LOW KEY at 1515. We were ready for him. We had the anchor up and we motored over to the first lock where we side tied to . . . a French boat. Well, French Canadian anyway. The plan was for them to tow us through the first set of locks. I have had some rough experiences with French cruisers who have a reputation for either being horrible or wonderful people. This seemed like a perfect start to our transit—if you're writing about it. It was a train wreck waiting to happen. Unfortunately for the story, they turned out to be the mostly good kind of French.

There were four cruising boats that would head up the locks together that night to Lake Gatun. Two boats side tie and then each boat sends their outside lines ashore to the canal line handlers which secure the lines to large bollards. By the time we got into the first lock, it was night time. I had never transited at night. It was very cool. Locking up at night added a certain edge, transforming our transit into an almost medieval experience.

A big ship pulled into the lock ahead of us. The first two-boat raft pulled in and secured their lines. The French boat side towed LOW KEY in and then we secured to the sides. The big doors, pushed by gigantic hydraulic rams, slowly closed behind us. There was no turning back. Alarms went off and the water started to boil beneath us. It felt like a mild earthquake was rolling under my little home. Once the lock was filled, the parade made its way into the next lock starting the process over again. I could tell you that it was trying or stressful or that I feared for LOW KEY, but the truth is, I was pretty excited to be doing the canal on my own boat. As the helmsman on the towed boat, my job consisted of . . . doing nothing, so I had a beer. My crew knew what they were doing, the canal advisors on each boat orchestrated everything well, and our locking up to the lake went off without a hitch.

After the last lock, we made our way, again under tow, into the lake a-ways to side-tie to a giant round buoy. It must have been 15-feet across. Still rafted, we settled in for an evening of cockpit lounging. There was no wind. The lake was glass calm. There was no moon. The stars were brilliant. You could hear the sounds of the wildlife ashore. It was an amazing evening. There we were, 80 feet above sea level, in fresh water, just little LOW KEY and I and our very diverse crew. We shared pasta and wine and listened to Santana and Marley and told our very different stories. It was a night I will never forget.

Bright and early, our advisor arrived and started shouting, "let's go, let's go, let's go!" Very funny. I figured that we would have to either mellow this guy out or pitch him over the side. He would tell us later that we were reported to be the slowest boat and that it was his job to hurry us across the great waterway in time to lock down with the other boats. They were right, I couldn't keep up with the other boats . . . under power. At the first opportunity, I asked if I could hoist some sail. He gave me an ecstatic, "Yes!" The favorable wind lasted about five minutes and then turned onto the nose for the rest of the 40-mile trip. I would not soon be catching up with the fat, big-motored cruisers ahead.

It was a beautiful transit though. The middle portion of the canal is amazingly lush. Every now and then we would pass a big ship coming the other way. We were warned to not leave the buoyed lane even though the lake was very deep. "Petrified trees," it was explained to us. When they flooded the lake they left the trees on each side of the traffic lanes. They have since turned rock hard and do a lot of damage when boats hit them. We had George, our advisor, pick out some music and we cranked it up. Before long George was getting his groove on, dancin' to Aretha and generally enjoying the ride. I broke out the deck chairs on the bow and James and I kicked back a few coldies as the incredible scenery rolled by.

On the other side of the canal we rafted up again with our

French friends and locked three times down. After spilling out the bottom, we pulled up to a tug and dropped off George. It had been a year since I had last been in my ocean, the vast Pacific. It smelled like home. We took a mooring at the Balboa Yacht Club. Everyone packed up their things and we made our way ashore. One by one, I thanked and bid farewell to my new sailing friends. And then, once again, LOW KEY and I were on our own.

CHAPTER 21

Back in the Pacific

I was in Balboa, Panama. I had just transited the Panama Canal. It felt pretty good to be back in the ocean I was raised on. After having a full boat of crew during the canal, it was nice to be alone with LOW KEY. Sitting peacefully on the mooring off Balboa, I thought back to all the adventures we had experienced together and thanked her for taking me to all the wonderful places we had been.

The push to California would be a long one. I had other cruisers insisting that I sail out to Hawaii and tack back, that trying to head straight up the coast against wind, current and swell was self-inflicted torture. About the third time I heard this, I decided to give the advice its fair consideration. A few seconds later I reconfirmed my plan to bang up the coast.

I went into Panama City and had a look around. There were some bigger buildings and more people, but it hadn't changed much since I'd been there last. Back at the dock they had set up an impromptu roadside "yacht club" overlooking the spot where the old one had burnt down. The original yacht club was a grand old building that hung on the edge of the steep hill that overlooked the moorage and boats from everywhere. As with all real yacht clubs, voyaging mariners were always welcome. I had many good times in the old club and was sorry to see it gone.

Up the road from the new club was a TGI Fridays. I'm not

a huge fan of chain establishments, but with nothing else around, I let hunger lead me in for some food and a coldy at the bar. I met a cool older couple there that were headed south in a van. They had met in high school. He was her teacher. When the parents found out, it hit the fan and the pair headed south. After running drug boats in the Caribbean, they settled in Costa Rica where they had been managing a cruiser bar for the last 25 years. They told me that Costa Rica just wasn't as cool anymore. They had heard that there were parts of Ecuador that were like CR was in the 70s. They were headed that way. It's never too late for a new start.

I was hanging out at the new yacht club when I heard a familiar voice. I looked over and saw my old friend Captain Ron from NEVER NEVER LAND. I had met Ron and his wife Janice in Sydney Harbour over a year before. They were circumnavigating the wrong way in a 60' Hatteras. It was the wrong way for sailboats, but apparently it was the right way for big power boats. We had parted ways in Australia; they were headed east and we were headed west. The odds of bumping into them this way were staggering—another cruising small world story. I got invited to dinner on NNL the next night.

Dinghies are not allowed in the Balboa mooring field. The Yacht Club provides water taxis to service the mooring customers and give them a lift back to the pier. I had heard different stories on whether or not to tip the taxi drivers. If I had given a driver a tip already that day, I didn't tip him again. This worked great for a while. But of course, the one time I had an appointment, my dinner plans with NNL, the guy refused to pick me up. I had to launch the dinghy. The next day, when I was paying for my mooring at the office, I asked what the official stance was on tipping. The manager told me not to tip, that it was causing problems. I told him my story. I didn't see that taxi driver after that.

In Balboa there is a chandlery called the Marine Warehouse. Marcos runs the place, and if he doesn't have the marine item you are looking for, then he will have it sent in. Marcos also puts out a great Cruiser's Directory for Panama. To find out where you can pick up this free directory or to locate one of Marcos' stores, just e-mail: panama@marinewarehouse.net.

I was in Balboa checking on my laundry when I bumped into Dennis, uh oh. Yes Dennis, the American who runs Cartegena and delivers backpackers from Colombia to Panama on his big ketch. What he was doing in Balboa, I didn't know. My laundry wasn't ready and I really didn't have anything else to do that day and so . . .

Dennis and I started by going over to the liquor store and buying a bottle of rum, a couple of Cokes and two glasses. Dennis knew the guy behind the counter by name. There was a bar across the way that I had been wanting to check out. We walked in. It was a nice place but it was pretty dead. Dennis looked around. "What are you looking for, D?" I asked. He headed over to a door that had a big sign on it that said, "NO ADMITTANCE," and walked through it. I decided to follow him. Walking through that door was like walking back in time. I had been transported from the colorful restaurant into a mostly grey and smoke-stained beige Elk's Club. There were guys at the bar that looked like they had been sitting there for decades. They ignored us as we made our way over to the pool table, drinks still in hand. Dennis racked 'em up.

We spent a couple good hours at the Elk's Club playing pool, table shuffleboard and darts and watching Starsky and Hutch reruns. From there we cabbed to the casino downtown where I proceeded to lose a couple bucks at craps. It was a tapered down Panama version of craps where the odds of winning had been whittled to nada. After trying to win back my money at the blackjack table, we called it a night.

I was expecting my next crewmember sometime that evening. We returned from the casino to find Mike onboard LOW KEY amidst a pile of empty beer cans. Mike had made himself right at home. I liked him already. Dennis had heard of a place where we could procure an after-hours drink. Not thinking straight at this point, I agreed to check it out. I remember Dennis giving extensive instructions to the cab driver. I remember finally pulling up to a place, going inside, and having a drink.

I remember hearing Dennis ask, "Donde están las mujeres?" just as the door to the kitchen opened up, revealing a bright ray of sunlight coming through a small window. I went into auto-mode. I got up, walked out, went up the street a bit and got in a cab. I was raised by jackals, the kind of guys that could drink for three days straight, the kind of guys that could convince you to have just one more when you said that you really did have to leave this time. I had learned to just sneak away when I was done.

I made it back to the boat through the blinding sun and was just settling into my bunk when I heard a cop knock on the hull. You know the knock, obnoxious and too loud to be any of your friends. I arose to find the local policía standing in a water taxi with some crazed civilian. It turns out that the guy was a taxi driver and he wanted $60 for bringing Mike back from the bar. I asked the cops, in my worst Spanish, if the bar was on the moon. One of them smiled. I looked the cabbie in the eye, handed him a twenty and they all went away.

How did he know that Mike was on my boat? After Mike had given the guy all of his money and the guy wanted more, Mike escaped and swam out to the boat. He was hanging from the anchor chain during my interactions with the fuzz. We figured that the cabbie must have been the same guy we had all night and he had just kept the meter running. I'm sure Dennis was disappointed to find out that his private cab had taken off.

After a day of recovery including a visit to Immigration, Mike and I departed Balboa for Costa Rica. I had considered the canal to be one of my last big obstacles to completing my sail around the world. It was the only place on the planet where I had to rely on my engine. My Volvo had served me well. (In less discerning environments, when talking about my beloved engine, I pronounce it with an 'a' at the end.) I had had no major problems with it since I left California 30,000 miles prior. That being said, I hadn't used the motor much. I could count on one hand how many times I had refueled. When I did motor we would run at 4.3 knots. The prop may have been a bit small, but at that speed the engine had a minimum of vibration and just sounded right. The canal required a five-knot minimum. Prior to our transit, my canal concerns spawned a conversation between my Volvo and me. I promised it that if it got us through the canal I would ask no more of it. If we got through the canal we could sail back to California . . . theoretically. It was listening. After a perfect canal crossing, we started to have issues.

Costa Rica or bust

We had a nice start to the first leg of that long last beat to California. After a long, hot sunny day of motoring, the clouds came in and gave us some relief. Mike had brought down one of those iPod things with a thousand songs to help the time pass. I could see though that Mike was having trouble adjusting to the heat. "Can we open the front of the dodger?" he asked as he pawed the frozen zippers.

"I'm afraid not," I said and explained that I had sealed them with silicone to keep the water out. I had learned that hard lesson in the fury of the Southern Indian Ocean. But Mike would never see big seas or a rough beat during his visit to LOW KEY. Our sail to Quepos in Costa Rica was mostly a motor through flat water. I was relieved to have put off the beating that I knew would eventually come. I think Mike was disappointed. He was fired up to do some real sailing. We did get to see a lot of other cool stuff. I awoke one morning to the sound of surf. I checked Mike's course on the GPS. He was right on. As the sun came up I could see the breakers pounding the beach off Punta Mala. We had dolphins visit us there, the kind with the grey backs. I thought back to all of the different sizes and colors of dolphins that I had seen on my trip. These ones were the kind you find in the Pacific.

About a day out of Quepos, I noticed that my (previously slight) wobble in the drive shaft was now getting worse. The wobble was letting more water in through the packing. Option A: Pull the shaft out and have it straightened or replaced somewhere—a tall order in the third world and with a guest onboard. Option B: Break rule #1 on a cruising boat and ignore it . . . for now. I went with option B; the bilge needed a good rinse anyway. We sailed when we had wind and in the calms we motored. That night we caught a nice skipjack on the handline just in time for dinner. We cooked it up in a lemon garlic butter marinade and washed it down with a couple of coldies. What more could you want?

And finally we arrived in Quepos. I love Costa Rica, home of tacos, *ticas* and tall beers. We anchored off the beach. Before heading ashore, I zoomed over in the dink to rescue a fishing *panga* that was drifting into the surf. This was a good way to start our visit to this cool little fishing village. Mike and I hit the town, got checked in, and had a look around. We ended up at a place called Dos Locos, which seemed appropriate. At closing time the bar/restaurant presented us with a bill for 172,000. It turned out not to be dollars, it was in colones. We made some jokes before attempting the math to figure out how much it was in dollars. I asked the owner if she had a calculator. I think she misunderstood because she went away and returned with an angry chef. He got into a little argument with Mike and soon . . . you guessed it . . . the cops were there. When you get a check in Costa Rica, don't hesitate, don't joke around, just pay the bill. Mike and I had figured out by this time that between us, we didn't have enough money. I asked the cops if they could direct me to the nearest ATM. The policía not only gave us a lift but offered to take the money back to Dos Locos for us. How nice is that?

To celebrate our not getting arrested for the second time in two countries, I dragged Mike over to a nice bar around the corner to meet up with some Euro backpackers that I had met earlier. As Mike tells it, I ended up making out with one of the girls in the bar while Mike talked to the second girl and her boyfriend. I don't remember if that's the way it went down, but it would explain the really friendly e-mail I got a couple days later from some girl whose name I didn't recognize.

My next crewmember, Dennis (a different Dennis), arrived the next day. That evening, Mike's family tracked him down.

They had come down to do some land-based traveling with him in Costa Rica. There was a big fishing tournament in town that weekend, so Mike's family was having a hard time finding a room. Dennis offered them his room and stayed on the boat that night. It worked out perfectly.

Dennis booked onboard LOW KEY for the leg from Quepos to Huatulco, Mexico. I wanted to try and make the 800-mile sail in one shot. We wanted to check out of Costa Rica. Dennis got to see a third world check-out procedure first hand. Immigration sent us to the Port Captain who told us we could not check out of the country from Quepos. She told us to sail to Puntarenas to check out. I thanked her and we left. Dennis wanted to know what Puntarenas was like. I told him we were not going there. Puntarenas was way up inside a long bay and it was mileage I didn't want to make. We would head to Playa del Cocos. Cocos held some memories for me, most of them good. It was in Cocos that I first ran with the bulls at the Costa Rican version of a rodeo. It was also in Cocos that Bob Bitchin got thrown in jail and then sent off to prison only to be rescued by a CIA agent. You think I'm kidding? I was there and met the agent when he returned Bob to us. Bob wrote it up in his book, *Letters from the Lost Soul.*

We left Quepos motoring. The shaft wobble didn't seem worse, though we did develop a fuel leak. I pulled the top off the manual fuel pump and cleaned it up and swapped the original gasket with a big O-ring I had. Dennis warned me that the rubber O-ring might not hold up to the corrosive fuel. I gave him the "make-do with what you got" speech. He was right of course.

We arrived in Potrero, otherwise known as Playa Flamingo, in the blackest part of the night. I detailed to Dennis the long list of reasons to not go into a strange harbor at night before I turned the boat and headed into the dark abyss. LOW KEY and I were in our element. We hadn't seen much excitement in the last couple months and so we took advantage of this break from the mundane. Still, we were careful. We came in slow and watched the depth sounder. There was a shallow spot in the bay that we had to get by. I kept us near shore under steep cliffs on which the bright vacation homes sat. My ancient cruising guide said that there was a marina in Playa Flamingo, which meant a fuel dock. Deep inside the bay we found an unlit breakwalled entrance to what looked like a marina. Instead of waiting for morning, I decided to head in now and tie up to the fuel dock and wait for it to open. We pulled in slowly as we watched the depth come up to eight feet. Inside, it was clear that the marina had long been abandoned. I also discovered that the marina had not been dredged in a long time. The bottom was coming up fast. With no room to maneuver, we had to back out. Safely at anchor, we toasted our survival of another treacherous journey, had some arrival popcorn, and passed out.

In the morning we dinked into the other marina. It wasn't abandoned but it was equally run down. The "Marina Flamingo" sign at the top of the dock had real vultures hanging all over it. That about summed up the place. We had to top up the fuel for the upcoming crossing of the deadly Bahia Tehuantepec. With no known fuel docks in northern Costa Rica, this was our last chance. We met Roberto who had one of those cool little car/trucks, self painted, sparkly blue. Roberto knew a guy who lived in the Brazilian part of town and owned a big 30-gallon container. With the container we could drive a half an hour to the gas station and get our diesel. I could adopt Roberto and his plan for a scant $30. I haggled to no avail. Roberto had me and he knew it.

Arriving back at the dock we somehow got the fuel container into the dink and out to the boat. With the mainsheet we hoisted the fuel container aboard. We gravity-fed the fuel into the fill in the cockpit and into the tanks. With the container back ashore and Roberto paid, we ambled up to the Spreader Bar above the "Marina." With coldies in hand, Dennis wanted to know if fueling was usually that . . . involved. "Not just fueling, Dennis, everything takes longer in cruising." I explained that it was O.K. because you have the time. If you can achieve one project a day then you should be happy, and I was. Here we were in this great little backpacker bar with a swimming pool overlooking the bay, fueling done, sucking down coldies, and it wasn't even three o' clock.

Long days in paradise

We sailed around the point that afternoon to Playa del Cocos. We anchored up close to shore. There was some kind of fiesta happening and so we went in for some roadside stand grub and refreshments. Back at the boat, I stayed up late writing in the cockpit with that very cool Flamenco-type music drifting out from shore.

The next morning, we went ashore to visit the Port Captain. The good news was that he could give me a zarpe, the piece of paper that allows you to check into the next country. The bad news was that because of the four day festival I had to wait until Monday for the bank to open to pay the fee. I could see where this was heading. No problem, I told him. I would just give him the money, I didn't need a receipt, and I would take my zarpe and be on my way. As it turns out, I was dealing with the one honest Port Captain in Latin America. I had heard about him. I thought he was a myth. He wasn't looking for some extra cash. He was just trying to do his job properly. I thanked him.

So there we were, stuck in one of the coolest beach towns in all of Costa Rica, for the long weekend. It was a much needed respite from the go go attitude that I had been maintaining to get the boat home in time. In time for what, you ask? I had tentatively scheduled my arrival back in the states for the middle of May. Then I heard that *Latitudes & Attitudes* was organizing a big Share the Sail charter and Eric Stone Concert in Tonga, scheduled to depart just before then. I decided to get home a little early so that Bob would at least have the option of sending me on the Tonga gig. Other cruisers had been telling me that my original schedule was not realistic, and so this new earlier arrival date would be a fun challenge for me.

We needed water. I went up to one of the big beach houses with a hose out front. I explained my situation to one of the guys standing there. He said he had to ask the owner. The owner said yes but that the good drinking water was on the other side of the property. He sent his daughter out to help me. Young Marisia, in a bikini, walked me through the grounds of the estate while practicing her nearly perfect English. It was like a scene out of one of those "this will never happen to you" movies. After walking me back to the beach she said, "Now please come back anytime." I wondered how Dennis would take it when I broke the news to him that I was moving in with Marisia and her family.

I finished up the watering and met up with Dennis on the beach. Dennis was sitting at the edge of the road with his head in his hands. Dennis had called home and learned that his best friend had died suddenly. I thought about what it must be like to find out something like that while you're away. It must be terrible. Dennis found a flight out that day and left us.

Interesting how your whole situation can change in a matter of minutes. I was no longer in a rush to get to Huatulco to meet up with Dennis's flight. I could fix the shaft problem here in cool little Cocos and skip Huatulco altogether, to make up the time.

I got right on it. The locals I was talking to were saying that straightening or replacing a prop shaft couldn't be done. I found gringo Ed who had a machine shop behind Cocos' mini chandlery. He told me, "Bring it in, we'll get 'er done." Ed knew about a place in Puntarenas, the place we bypassed (oops), that made prop shafts cheap.

Diving under the boat I quickly figured out that the shaft wouldn't come out of the back of the boat without hitting the rudder skeg. And so I pulled the engine out and set it on the settee in the saloon. I had to use two block and tackles from the boom to lift the 300 pound leviathan and there were electrical, water, drive shaft and exhaust systems that had to be disconnected. That stuff didn't worry me. The hard part of the operation would be after putting the engine back in and going through the extensive alignment process. And all this while parked in a rolly roadstead anchorage. On the plus side . . .

how fun is it to work on your engine while it is sitting in front
of you, pivoting around on its oil pan? Everything is super accessible. I got a little sidetracked for a couple of hours, checking stuff out and cleaning and rebuilding stuff.

I pulled the shaft out. Emotionally, I wasn't prepared to
see that much water pour into the boat from such a small hole.
It took me by surprise. I suppose it is a good instinct to be
concerned about something like that. I put the wooden plug in
and then wired it to the packing gland, just in case. Pulling the
engine out had broken the two aft engine mounts. I suspect
they had been weakened by the wobble. I took the shaft, the
engine-to-shaft coupling, and the mounts in to Ed. He was out
fishing on the day we were supposed to meet. Luckily,
Rosendo was there. Rosendo was born in Costa Rica but lived
in Southern California for most of his life. We figured out that
the shaft was straight and that it was the shaft-to-coupling
mate that had worn down. Rosendo knew a place that could
"fix" it.

We took a bus to the "big" town of Liberia, dropped my
broken pieces off at Federico's super machine shop, ran some
other errands for Rosendo, and bussed back to Cocos. A couple days later I picked up my "new" parts ($92) and bused
back. En route, I did get a nice shot of the jungle prison that
Bob Bitchin had "visited" on our last trip through here. Blow it
up, slap it in a frame . . . I smell a birthday present.

It took three hours, all told, to get the shaft out of the
boat. It took about twice that to get everything back together.
I cheated on the alignment a little. I left the engine hanging on
its hoists so I could lift it and turn the adjustment nuts by
hand when needed. There was other work done on LOW KEY
that weekend. I was getting a crack around the base of the
tiller in the cockpit. I chipped away the glass and filled it with
an epoxy mix—better than new. I had the epoxy out so I rebuilt the deck under a leaky stanchion base. With the engine
out, the lifelines down and the tiller off, I felt a little uncomfortable. I wasn't safely tied up at a marina. I was in an anchorage just off a beach with surf. I had put my stern hook off

the bow as a back up to the heavier main anchor. As soon as the engine was back in and running, I retrieved the spare anchor. I don't like having two anchors out. It can make a quick departure complicated.

With the big jobs completed, I showered on deck in the dark of night between the Southern Cross and the North Star. After a nice meal, I motored out of the bay, the shaft turnin' straight, a first since I have owned LOW KEY. The wind never came up that night. Nessie can only steer for me if there's wind to drive her. At 0100 I shut down the big diesel and drifted. I slept deeply until 0600. I took up sailing just so I could get to the great destinations. More recently I really started to like the sailing for the sailing. Just being at sea fulfills me. When we're anchored we are interacting with the ground, the shore, the local people and other boats. Adrift in the ocean we are free. It's just about us and the sea and interacting with her creatures.

Battle in the Tehuantepec

I got an e-mail from Bob telling me that his film crew would be in Huatulco in five days. I was 700 miles from there. That would be easy in a downhill tradewind situation. That wasn't the case. I hadn't yet committed myself to pulling into Huatulco. To get there I would have to cut into the dreaded Bahia Tehuantepec, an odd stretch of water where winds can pipe up to 100 knots on a clear day. I was aiming for a spot 250 miles offshore thinking that if the winds did come up they might be less offensive that far out.

As I approached the big bay, my smail grib files were telling me that a minor Tehuantepecer was brewing. Only 40 knots was forecast. LOW KEY is too light to beam reach in 40 knots. We would have to turn tail and bare-pole downwind for a while. That seemed acceptable to me. I stayed on course and eased into the mouth of the 200-mile bay. We were on schedule for a rendezvous with Bob's crew.

Then the wind shut off—the calm before the storm? I fired

up the engine. I forgot to check the exhaust. There was a clog somewhere in the raw water cooling system. No water was running through the engine. I fried the muffler. I shut down and drifted. I radioed a passing container ship to check on conditions in the bay. He told me that it was rough for him. I smiled my friends Chuck and Ann who had their boat in Huatulco at the time. They got back to me and said that I had a couple of days to make it before the next Tehuantepecer came through.

I got on the muffler repair. I was out of the good epoxy. I improvised. I filled the holes with silicone gasket maker and then tied a rag around that. I secured the rag with exhaust tape. I let it set up . . . for 20 minutes and then fired her up. I was getting a water drip but the exhaust was going outside. I could live with that.

I motored fast now. The wind would come up now and again and I would leave the engine on for extra speed. I was hitting eight knots upwind which was fast for LOW KEY. I picked up a passenger. A lone blue-footed boobie landed on the end of the boom before moving into the cockpit next to me. Those birds are fearless. It took some pushing and shoving and snapping beak avoidance, but I got Freddie to sit on the rail where the inevitable mess would be easier to clean up. Chuck smailed me again, telling me how cool Huatulco was, how great the marina was, how I could get clean fuel there and that the first coldy was on him. Does a cruiser need to hear more? I turned the bow a little more to starboard, into the danger zone but closing the gap to safety faster.

I finally spotted land. I was a day late and I wondered if I had missed the film crew. I smailed Chuck again but received no response. Hopefully he was working hard still entertaining the crew. As I closed with the harbor, Chuck came up on 16. It was good to hear his voice after two years. He put me on the radio with Enrique, the marina manager, who talked me in. As I scooted around the breakwall and dredging equipment, I spotted a group of people. Were they there for me? I pulled into my slip and was greeted by a bunch of smiling faces. I traded hugs with Chuck and Ann, got my coldy. Next I met young Shanna from the *Lats* TV show. I also met two other cruising couples there on the dock with whom I would soon become good friends. It was a wonderful way to come in after a long, sketchy trip.

CHAPTER 22

Coming Home

After a week at sea and a safe crossing of the deadly Bahia Tehuantepec, I made my first stop in Mexico at the small town of Huatulco. I was greeted by friends from home and soon-to-be friends. After getting cleaned up, Chuck and Ann of MIRAGE took me into town. We had a great meal of—you guessed it, Mexican food—and after years of living without it, my favorite beer, Pacifico. It was good to be in the cool little town, good to be with old friends, good to be living the life of a cruiser.

Huatulco had changed since I had visited with LOST SOUL, eleven years prior. The government, grooming Huatulco for mass tourism, had put in new roads, storm drains, parks and a great marina. It was in Marina Chahue that I parked. The place was very clean and organized, but the best part of it was the marina manager, Enrique. The guy was on top of everything and he was all about helping the cruising community.

The next day I was invited to the big motor yacht DELIA. Ricardo and crew asked me to join them for *comida*. Comida is the afternoon meal in Mexico. Comida usually has lots of meat in it. It had been a week since I had had some meat, so it was very welcome. With coldy in hand, I hung out on the foredeck of DELIA that afternoon and, through welder's glass, watched the eclipse.

As it is with cruising, you just arrive at a place, see your long lost friends, and then they have to leave. Chuck and Ann on MIRAGE were heading the opposite way from LOW KEY and me. They were headed for the canal. I bid them and my new friends on WOODEN DUCK farewell. I had made friends with Brent, another U.S. singlehander on the dock who was younger than I was, late twenties I'd say. Brent and I went in that night to the big nightclub. Papaya was where the vacationing elite from around Mexico hung out. After a few beers and a few shots, there were a few attempts at trans-border relations.

The next day was a lazy one. I did laundry on deck in the morning before Brent swung by to inform me that we were going to spend the afternoon having coldies under a palapa at the beach resort around the corner. First things first. A boat had come in that morning that had a cute New Zealand girl aboard with what looked like her parents. I would have been rude to not offer her a break from the family and invite her with Brent and me to the beach. The three of us sat in lounge chairs and enjoyed the afternoon, being served our drinks and food by the sea.

Customs, Health and Immigration had finally tracked me down. They arrived on the boat and did their thing. I thought it was great that they all came down to check me into Mexico, but of course my check-in would not be that easy. I had to go to the town of Santa Cruz to check in with the Port Captain, too. The Port Captain would not let me check in and out at the same time, so I had to come back the next day. On both trips I would be sent to the bank to pay fees. Nothing had changed in Mexico.

I prepped LOW KEY to leave the next day. Enrique, the world's coolest dockmaster, drove Brent and me into town to get diesel for our boats at the gas station. He even provided the containers. We had a BBQ on Brent's boat that night, hamburgers and all.

Bright and early, Ricardo and Delia came by to wish me a safe trip. Ricardo gave me a bottle of champagne to open when I finally returned to my home. I filled LOW KEY's water tanks and prepped her anchor and said goodbye to Brent and Enrique. I motored out of the dredge-strewn pass and dropped the hook off the beach so I could clean the bottom of the boat. With the boat clean and full of food, water, and fuel, I headed out to sea.

And so started the slog north

I had 1,656 nautical miles to go to reach San Diego. My plan was, well, I didn't really have a plan. I thought that I would just get out there and see what happened. The sea off southern Mexico was full of turtles, fish boils and rays. Enrique was saying how the Mexicans have been working hard to preserve the turtle egg-laying beaches. It was good to hear. Their efforts were paying off.

To leave this north edge of Bahia Tehuantepec, LOW KEY and I had to motor west first. We were headed into a slight wind. After rounding three points and making three course adjustments to starboard, LOW KEY and I were still motoring into it. The wind was following the coast.

One of the reasons I didn't want to hang out too long in Mexico was the deteriorating state of my little boat. Mostly, I was having engine problems. A gasket had hardened in my inaccessible manual fuel pump and it had started leaking. Tightening the hard-to-get-to bolts would work for a couple days at a time. One thing I couldn't fix was an oil leak that had developed low on the case. On deck, that first night, I found a broken wire on the port lower stay. This wasn't good. An Australian rigger had told me that with one broken wire you are usually O.K. With two wires it was time to head in. With three wires broken, you should take some sail down or tack over. Still, I was getting ready to do the Baja bash and didn't want to give the sea any advantage. The next day I pulled out an old lower I had stashed and changed out the weakened shroud. This meant a trip half way up the mast. It was pretty flat where I was at sea. All went well.

That night, my radar detector went off while I was below. I came up on deck to see a very large, unlit ship cruise by my port side. It happens. Another thing that happens is that you hit stuff. It doesn't happen that often, but where there are lots of turtles in the water. . . . It usually happens at night. It will be pitch black and you'll hear the bump at the bow and maybe another bump on the side as the turtle flails to get its bearings. Sometimes you'll see them during the day and can avoid them. Often there is a bird sitting on their back and so they are easier to spot. I hit one during the day; it came out the back unharmed as usual, but it did look kinda mad.

The wind finally came around to the beam. I put the whomper up and reached up the coast. With the engine off, I could hear so much more. I was about a mile off the coast when I heard tribal drums and jungle music and yelling far off in the distance. Ashore the land was thick green with a grove of palms near the water. A smoky haze covered the area. I could see no buildings. My imagination took over as I relived my fantasy of discovering French Polynesia 100 years before the Europeans arrived.

I got an smail from Tania Aebi. She just wanted me to be sure and enjoy the last part of my adventure. She was right. In pushing the boat home, one could get distracted and forget to appreciate where I was and what LOW KEY and I had done.

I eventually lost the wind and had to fire up the beast. I motored until dark and then some. Without wind to drive her, Nessie won't steer, so at about ten at night, I shut off the engine and, in a silent flat calm, I drifted off to sleep. After a few hours I woke up and added oil to compensate for the leak and fired the engine back up. My engine never used oil before, so I only carried enough for one oil change. I carried 100 hours of fuel and that always coincided with the oil change. Now that it had a small leak, I would have to pull in before I needed fuel. Later that day I would write in my log, "I don't know what's worse, beating into big seas/wind or having to motor and deal with maintenance, steering, fuel stops, noise and fumes. Remind me I said this off Baja."

Just for fun . . . I was out of both Marine Tex and the hardware store epoxy that came in the tube that I liked, and so I busted out the JB weld and tried to seal the leaky seam in the engine case. I tacked into light winds and a big current all day while the JB hardened. You guessed it, it didn't work. During this part of the trip I was doing 50- to 80-mile days. I could have taken crew from shore and motored day and night pulling in every 100 hours for fuel, but I wanted to do this last section of the trip by myself. Flipping through the log, I would see old entries with 140-mile days and wondered if those days were gone for good. I beat against current in light winds and motored through calms for so long, I was beginning to forget how I had sailed most of the way around the world in breezy downwind conditions.

I was approaching Acapulco. I wanted to make it to Zihuatanejo before stopping for oil and fuel. I tacked in near Acapulco Bay at sunset, waved to no one in particular, and tacked back out. It got dark fast. I saw then why the cruising guide called the night view of the bay from the sea "the bowl of diamonds."

I had made only 300nm in the last five days. The tacking in light air during the day was easy compared to keeping the boat straight while motoring through the nightly calms when I was very tired. Sometimes, after a long night of hand steering, I would look back on my GPS track and see a line traveled that wasn't always straight. I could have pulled into any of many ports but I was trying to keep to a minimum the excessive port paperwork that was always required. It was easier just to stay at sea and knock out a few more miles. Finally I was getting close to Zihuatanejo. The cruising guide explained how Zihuatanejo was once considered the western paradise of goddess women. Like I needed another reason to pull into there.

I arrived in Zihuatanejo at 0200. Towns always look their best at night. Happy for the break in the action, I got the anchor down and passed out. I checked into the town bright and early. The guy let me check in and out at the same time, though I still had to visit the bank ($34). I visited an Internet place way up inside the cool little town. Oddly, four of the most beautiful Mexican girls I had ever seen were checking their e-mail in that little building. Maybe there was something to this legend. I found oil and bought new shoes—I mean, flip flops. I had lunch at La Sirena Gorda by the water.

Back at the boat, I tightened the screws on the manual fuel pump, changed the oil and filters, packed up the boat for sea, and headed over to take fuel. After fueling I motored out of the bay into a calm sea. Anticipating a long hard night of hand steering with no sleep, I turned around and anchored off a beach close to the entrance to the bay. It was nice there. I was ahead of schedule. I showered on deck and had a couple of sunset coldies under the cliff-side mansions. After a nice dinner, I watched a movie.

The good thing about parking in an open roadstead is that you know when the wind comes back up. I could feel the swell starting to roll into the bay before I got the wind. I pulled the hook and drifted out with the tide while I prepped the deck and sails. I was in Zihuatanejo for 26 hours—it seemed like a week.

For the next few days, the breeze would come from aft in the morning and swing around to the bow by nightfall before shutting off altogether. I wanted to make Cabo my next stop, but since the wind kept dying at night, I pulled in to fuel at Barra Navidad. It was at Barra that Dena and I departed the west coast of the Americas to cross the South Pacific almost two years prior. Just before arriving at Barra, I crossed our outgoing track, officially completing our circumnavigation. I congratulated my little boat. I thought back to the people who told me that you couldn't circumnavigate in an old Cal 33. My little boat had shown them.

I didn't mark it in my log book for fear of getting in trouble with the Mexicans, but I pulled into Barra Navidad for fuel and then just left. I called the Capitan del Puerto on the radio when I entered but got no response. I could not see spending the day running around and paying another $37 for a half-hour visit to the fuel dock. It's something I'll have to live with. I haven't lost any sleep over it.

I've said it before: Barra is one of my favorite Mexican stops. It has the world's nicest marina setup. The marina is super protected and clean, but that's not what makes it special. The marina there is attached to an amazing hotel. The hotel lets the boaters hang out at the pools that cascade down from the north to south. The three pools are connected by mini water slides. When you get tired of hanging out poolside, head over to the water taxi dock where a panga will take you across the river to one of the coolest little towns in all of Mexico. The place has shacks selling arts and crafts and a couple cruiser hangouts, but it also has beachfront restaurants where you can enjoy a great meal while you watch the sun ease into the sea. You don't have to stay at the expensive marina. Hundreds of boats anchor in the "lake" every year.

After fueling and taking a couple of pictures, I headed back out into the light, a sailing by day and motoring by night routine. That night, another ship went by close-to on the port side. This one had lights on but no radar for me to pick up. Again, it was just lucky that I happened to be on deck at the time. My routine included sailing in toward shore during the day and watching the sunset cast pretty colors on the land in the evening before tacking out into the safety of deep water at night. Unfortunately this had me crossing the shipping lanes twice a day. I knew when to watch. I broke the "1,000nm to go" barrier that night. It was also the first time I felt the need to break out a sweatshirt since Cape Town.

My friends in Huatulco had given me the SSB frequencies for Don on SUMMER PASSAGE. Don was a cruiser, now land based, who researched and broadcast the weather a couple times a day on the SSB. Guys like Don are unbelievable with their knowledge and dedication to the weather—all for free. It's like watching Fritz on TV (is he still on?), but then being able to call him up and get a personal weather forecast for your area. Don was predicting more wind for my area. I was now between Puerto Vallarta and Cabo. At 0400 the wind shut off again, but this time there was a short swell rolling through and you know what that means—wind coming.

The moon was still up and full as the sun came up. The wind came up too, and we started a beautiful sail on a beam reach. It was sleep time but, as happens in Mexico (and I've heard it in Spain), there were Mexicanos playing on the VHF emergency channel, endlessly whistling and cursing in Spanish. I was crossing the entrance to the Sea of Cortez, a traffic area, and so I opted to leave the radio on, giving up some sleep.

The beating

LOW KEY and I were almost south of Cabo when the wind came on and stayed. It was blowing out of the sea and so I was flying to windward, hitting the odd 6 knots VMG (velocity made good), just to port of my course. The sky was blue and we had normal looking clouds. It looked like the wind was going to stay for a while. As the wind and the current slowly came around onto the nose, I quickly learned that in order to make any progress toward our destination, I would have to put up more sail than prudence would suggest.

LOW KEY is wide and flat on the bottom with a deep fin keel. These design attributes result in a very flat ride and fast downwind. With the excess sail up, LOW KEY, for the first time, was heeled way over and would stay that way for most of the bash. Looking back, I would say the middle part of the Indian Ocean crossing was more dangerous. The swells there were huge and constantly rolling over the boat. Off Baja, I never saw big swells, but I'm pretty sure that sailing into short swells is even more bumpy. The boat was doing 6 to 7 knots OG (over the ground), but because we were sailing west of our course, we were making only 2 to 3 knots toward our destination (VMG). LOW KEY would lift up for one swell, launch off the top, and come plowing down into the face of the next. There was a lot of slamming noises and rig shaking and hull flexing. After a couple of days I started getting used to it. The boat didn't seem to mind.

And the wind built. I was a 100 miles due south of Cabo when I woke up getting knocked around. We had too much sail up. Usually I would crack way off the wind for a sail change to keep the salt spray to a minimum, but here I didn't want to give up an inch. I changed down to the #3 headsail. I don't wear my harness as often as they tell me I should, but I strapped it on for that sail change. We were still banging hard but not giving up much. We were doing 2 knots VMG.

I had run out of eggs, which was O.K. because: a) I wouldn't be able to cook them in the ruckus and b) I wouldn't have to clean them off the floor when they inevitably launched themselves off the shelf. I had one onion left which I would slice a chunk from each day to use in my noontime noodles. It was noodles for lunch kind of weather. I would boil water in the kettle on the gimbaled stove and pour it over the noodles in a bowl, also on the stove, cover, and wait for 15 minutes. It was a bulletproof system that withstood the pounding of the boat. On the positive side of getting thrashed, we were at least sailing. With no engine on, I felt more comfortable sleeping below. I could hear what was going on so much better.

I was tuning into the morning nets and just listening, as opposed to participating by checking in. That would mean that I would have to get up at the same time everyday, which wasn't going to happen with my crazy schedule. I did decide that it was time to give weather guy Don a call and get my personal weather info. I was too far offshore to be covered by his daily synopsis of the weather on the net. Don was surprised to find me so far offshore. He suggested I come back in to the coast. The weather I was getting from him and Sailmail grib files both showed that there was always more wind along the coast. Mostly I was offshore because that is where the wind had taken me. To tack in would have turned my VMG to 0. There is of course a third option. Boats sometimes head 600 miles offshore to get to the other side of the high so they have a downwind run up to California. That would have worked for me too.

I passed the latitude of Cabo (west of Cabo) and the banging continued. As I maneuvered around inside the boat, I could feel the cold floor flexing under my feet. One morning I awoke to a tapping sound on the side of the hull. The sea had ripped my PVC rubrail back on the port side. Folded back, the end banged on the hull. While I was on deck tearing off that piece of rubrail, repair not an option, I could feel just how cold the water was. Which explains the need for sweats, and as of the night before, sea boots. With the barometer high and the presence of the cute little trade wind "Simpsons" clouds, I was looking at more of the same weather.

Just below Turtle Bay, half-way up Baja, I hit the two-year anniversary of our departure from LOW KEY's slip in Southern California. I tacked in toward the coast to see if I could lay Turtle Bay yet. The GPS told me no. I tacked back out. I didn't much like being near the coast anyway. It was always bumpier in there with the swells bouncing off the land. I wrote in the log that I was going down to attempt to do the dishes. Looking back, I don't remember it being so rough that something as simple as doing the dishes was difficult. I think that I selectively don't remember some of the not so fun aspects of the trip. Love is blind.

My weather guy Don was telling me that the high pressure system was moving in, which would mean lighter winds. I watched as the wind shifted west. This was good news. If I was finally getting on top of the high, then I would be getting a better wind direction. We had an 80-mile day that day. I decided to skip Turtle Bay. A visit to Turtle would have been fun, but I'm the type of person who wants to get the rough parts out of the way so I can get to the fun parts. Pulling in would have just been prolonging the beating.

The radar detector was going off again. I had a look—there was a tanker on the bow. I didn't want to tack; I had the boat set up just the way I wanted it and I was moving fast. I called the tanker on the radio. They didn't respond. This is typical. They hear you and then have a look for you and then decide whether they need to turn to avoid a collision. Often they never respond to you on the radio. The tanker VALIANT did get back to me, though. I clearly had right of way, but I've learned to not push the issue with large, hard-to-maneuver boats. I told him I was singlehanding and beating to weather. I finished with, "What would you like to do, Skipper?" He offered to

turn and turn he did. That huge boat turned 45 degrees in half
a minute. I suppose it was the speed that helped him turn. It
was impressive.

On approach

The wind dropped off again. I didn't care. I was within motoring range of San Diego, a couple of days out. I checked the oil
and fired up the engine. A couple of minutes later I smelled
smoke. Usually I can hear when the exhaust has no water running through it. I guess I was distracted. All of the hard sailing
had let air into the raw water intake for the engine, and the
pump couldn't get a prime. I melted the aqualift, the muffler, for
the last time. It was the last time because I had used up all of
the epoxy on previous fixes. I had, with my spares, one of those
gimmicky "repair your exhaust at sea" kits that included a
giant hose barb. I took the aqualift out of the system and connected the two hoses. The downside of taking out the aqualift
was the risk of seawater backing through the system and getting into the engine.

Dolphins are good luck, you know. I got them just south of
Ensenada, Mexico. The engine was purring and there was just
enough wind to make the windvane steering work. I cleaned up
the boat, e-mailed friends back home of my possible arrival,
and had a nice nap.

It was in the wee hours of the morning when I passed inside
Coronado Island. I could see the lights of the border and even
the Coronado Bridge. The sun came up and shined down on
San Diego. I could see Point Loma. It had been two years since
I had seen the U.S. I motored into the harbor and pulled up to
the harbor patrol dock where Customs would later come down
to meet me. It was a beautiful blue-sky sunny day.

After checking into my country, we sailed out again. LOW
KEY and I motored and sailed overnight to my own local cruising port of Two Harbors on the island of Catalina. We
splurged and took a mooring. I could have anchored out, but I

was ready to be around people after a couple weeks at sea. I had never had a nice boat of my own to visit my local island with. The weather was perfect with a slight chill. I dinked in and bellied up to the bar for a Buffalo Milk. It was starting— the checking off items from the long list of things that I had missed from home.

The Kentucky Derby was on the TV above the bar. A group of sailors there were placing bets. I got in on the action and met Orlando and Linda who were there with their sailing club. They had been reading about my adventures. I hadn't really thought about it. I had a deadline every month and sent the stories in, and people I didn't know were really reading them. They invited me to their beach BBQ that evening. It was a fun crowd and it was great to be around people.

The next morning, I got up and went ashore for the Mother's Day phone call, informing Mom that I would be home later that day. She might have been glad the thing was coming to an end. I also called my friend John to see if he could get me a temporary tie-up at his yacht club. I wanted LOW KEY to look her best, so I cleaned a couple weeks of growth off the water line. And then LOW KEY and I headed out to sea for the last time on this particular adventure.

I had almost forgotten. When I pull into a new country, I always turn on the radio to get caught up on some of the culture. This time I tuned into some of my old stations. That really brought back the feel of home. I had just rounded the big peninsula and could see my own King Harbor when I heard someone calling "LOW KEY" on the VHF. It was Bob Bitchin. A group of my friends were getting together on the big cat JANE O to come out and welcome me in. I met them at the entrance to the harbor. It was a great feeling to have made it home and to see all my friends so very excited for me.

I got LOW KEY parked and joined the party.